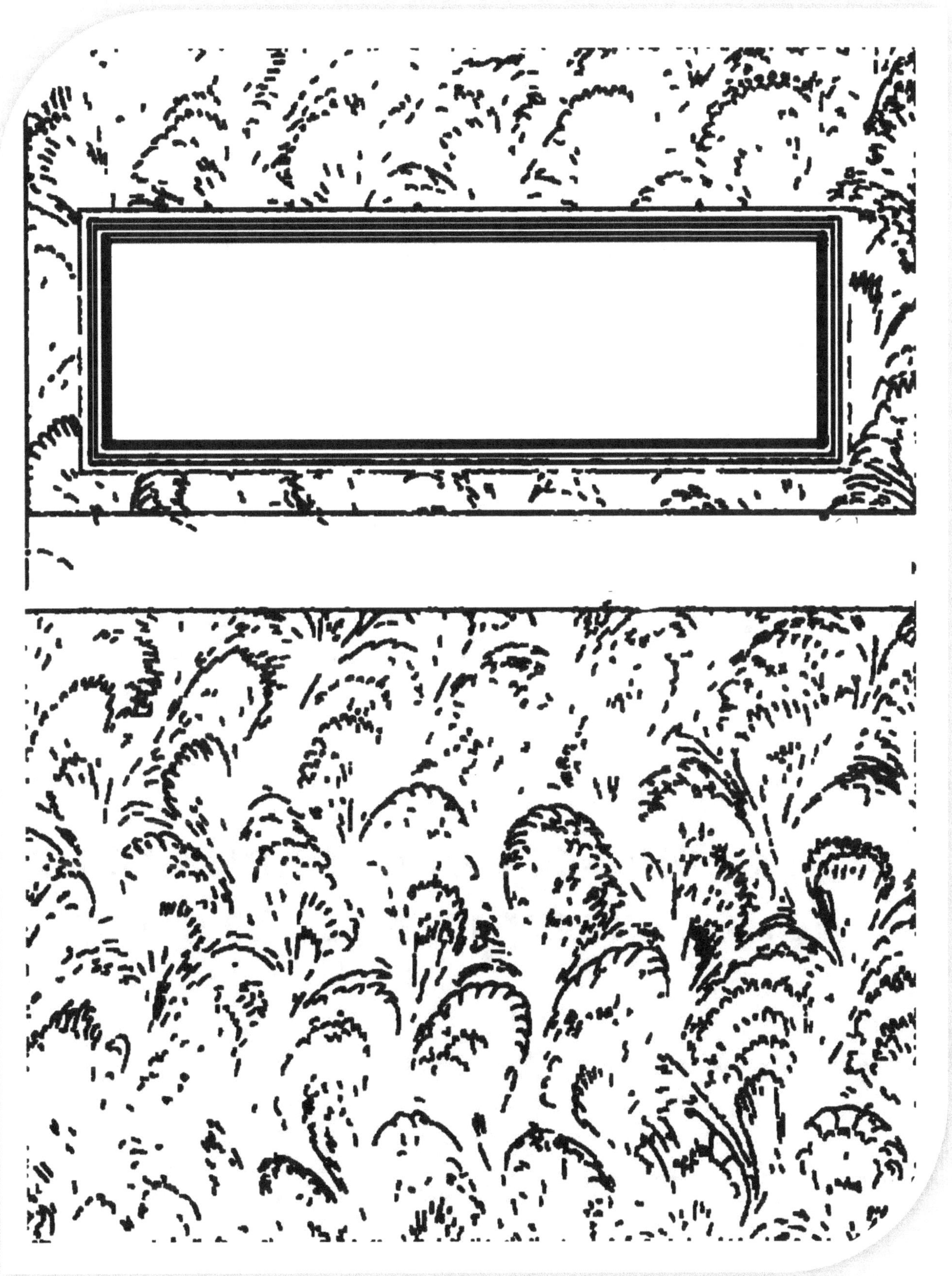

CRAYONS, COLORING PENCILS & PENS

COLORING BOOK 3

TRIBUTE TO ARTIST MINNIE EVANS SERIES
OF COLORING BOOKS

WELCOME
ENTER & COLOR

terrific, but very odd, hand drawn,
weird folk-art images to color

By Dr. Katie Canty, Ed.D.

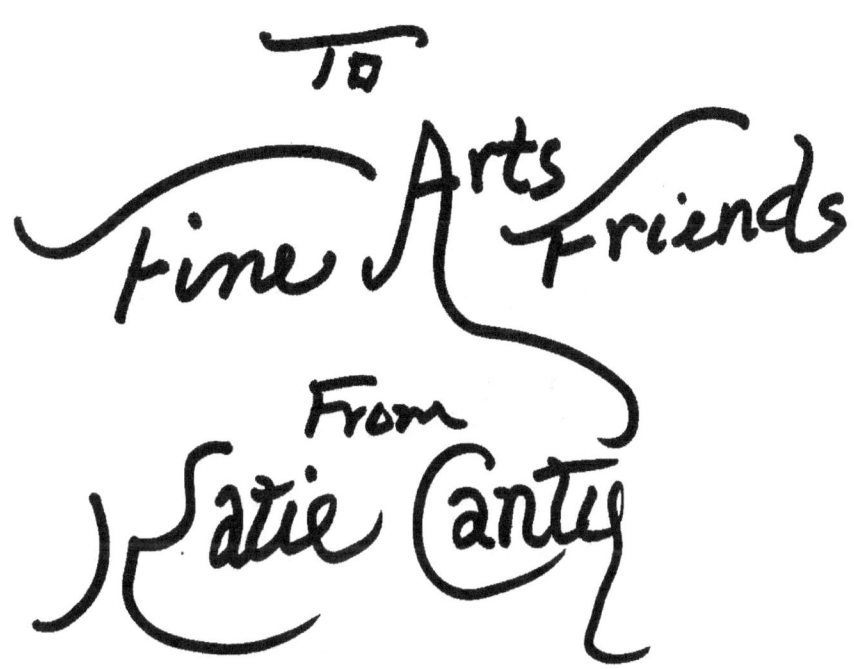

FIRST EDITION, AUTOGRAPHED

Copyright © 2018

ISBN-13: 978-1985798656
ISBN-10: 1985798654
Dr. Katie Canty, Ed.D.

DEDICATION

3D GREETING CARD ARTIST
JAIMEE CANTY

FINE ART & FOLK ART FRIENDS

CRAYON USERS EVERYWHERE

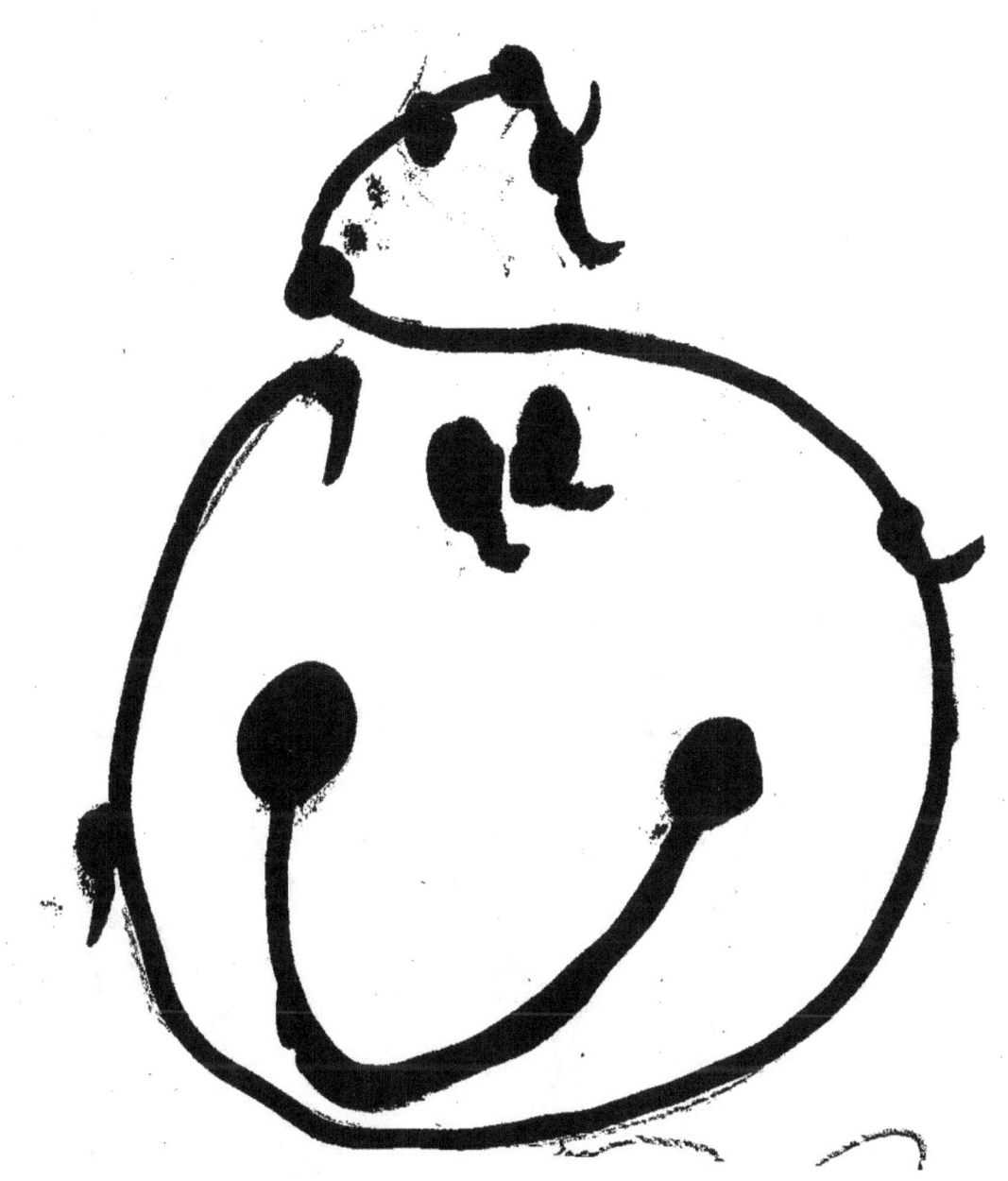

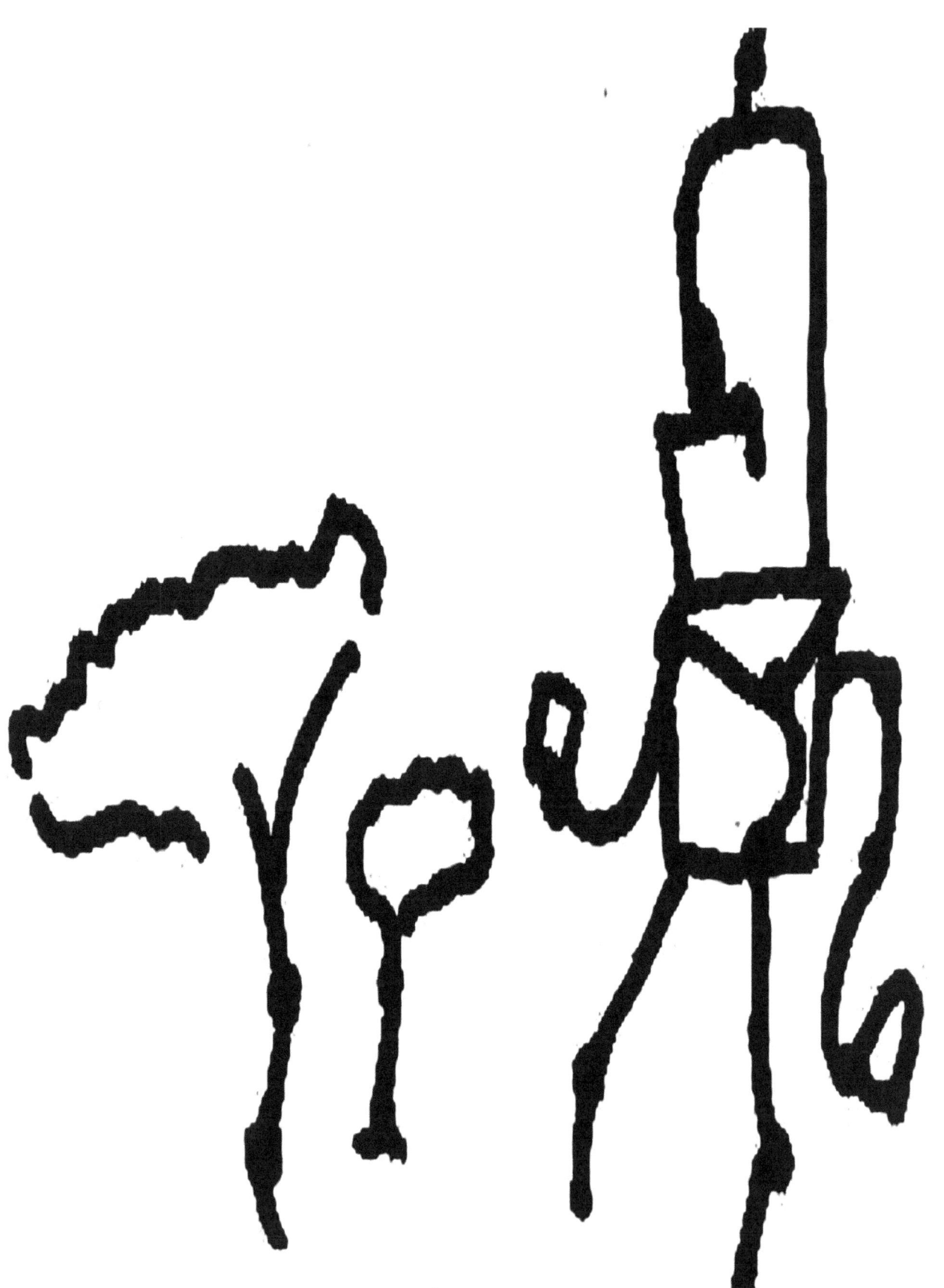

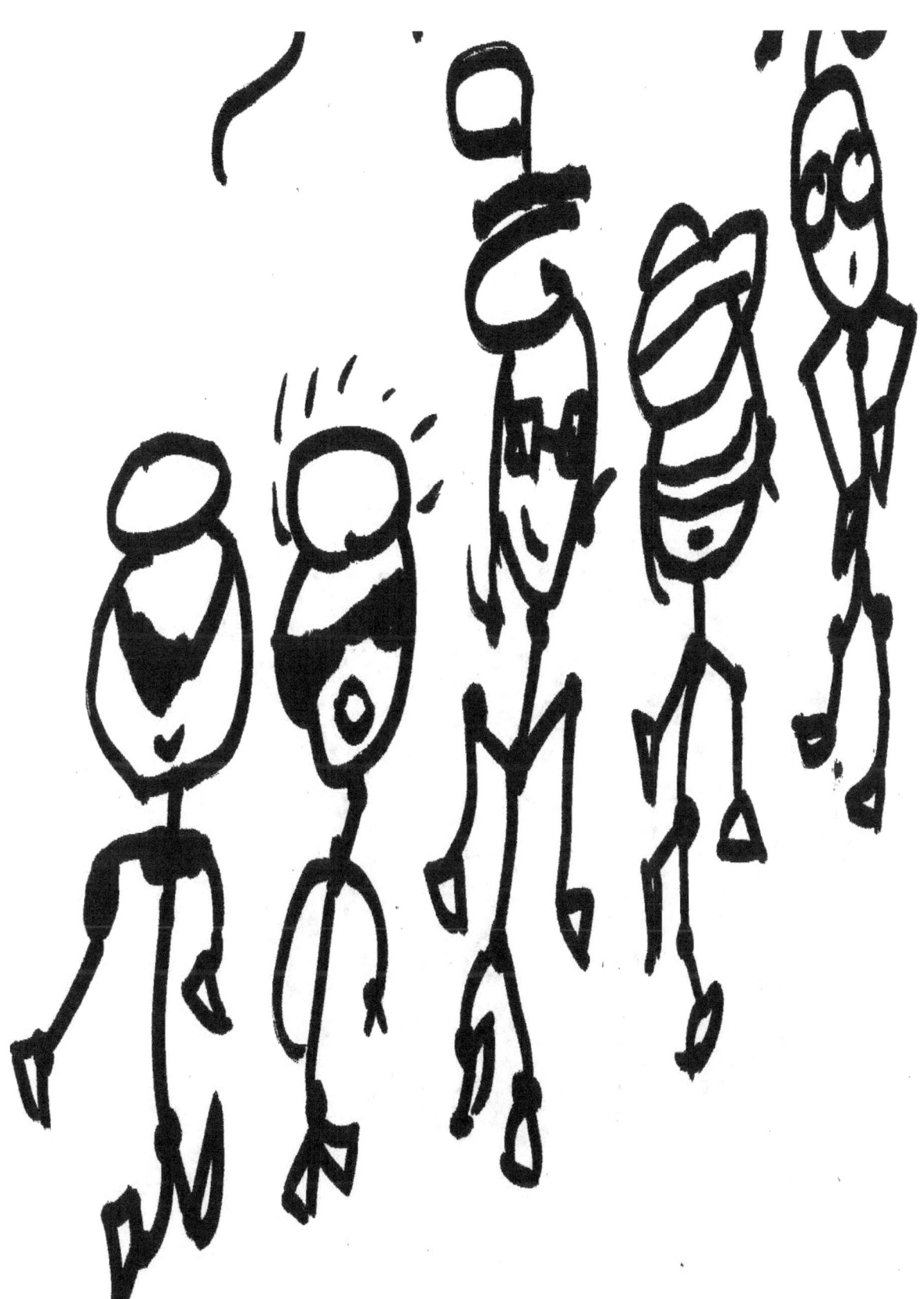

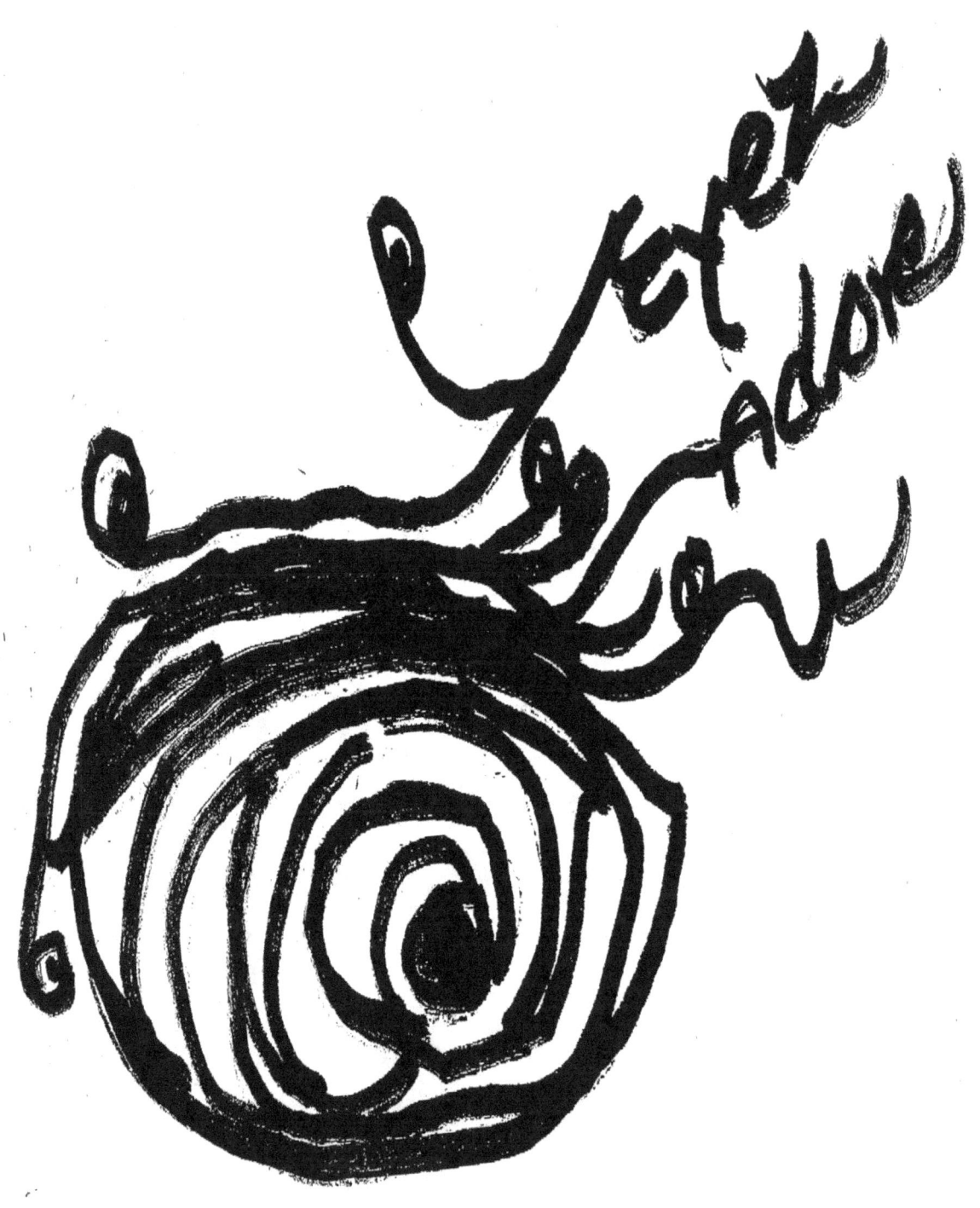

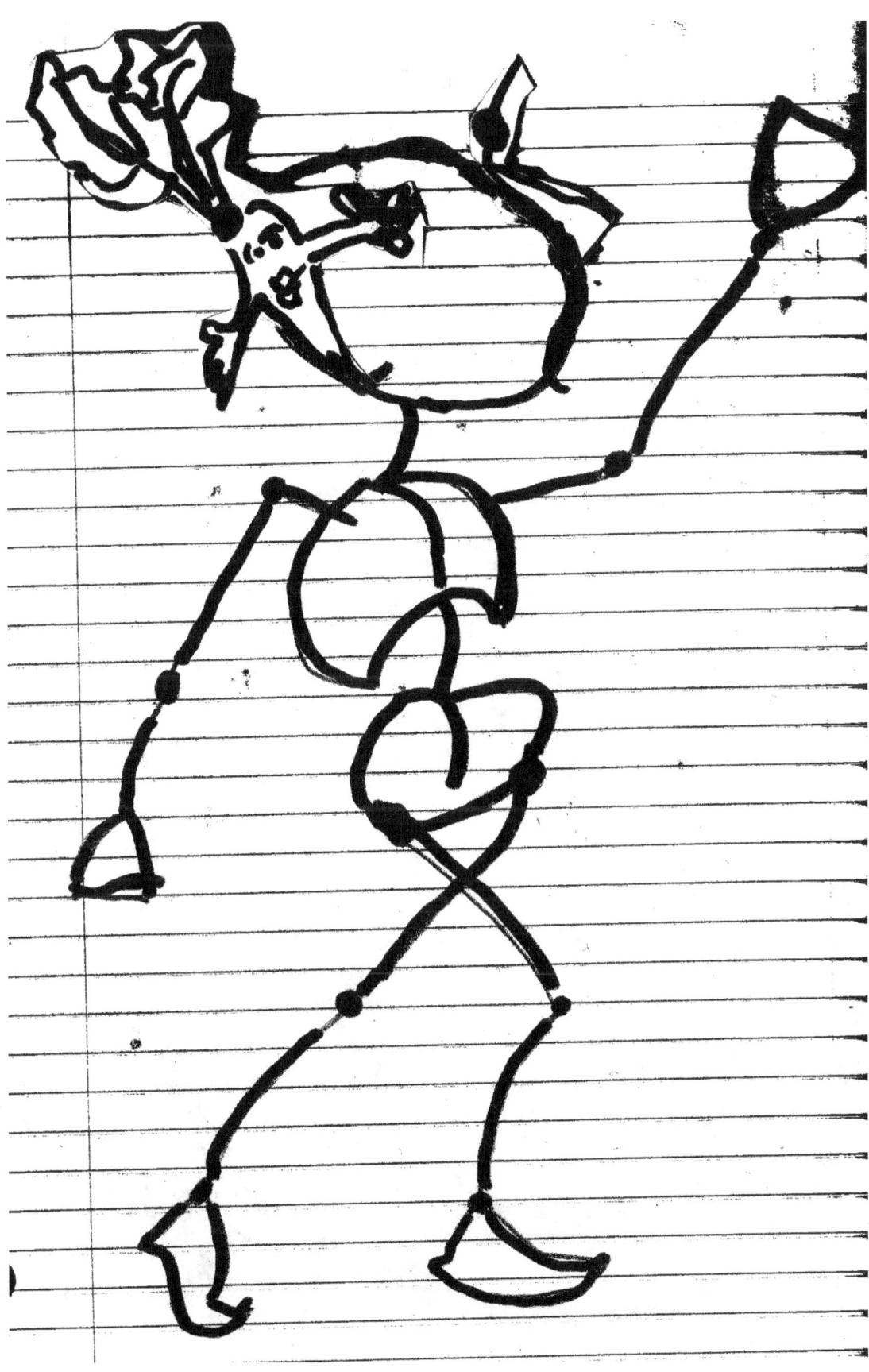

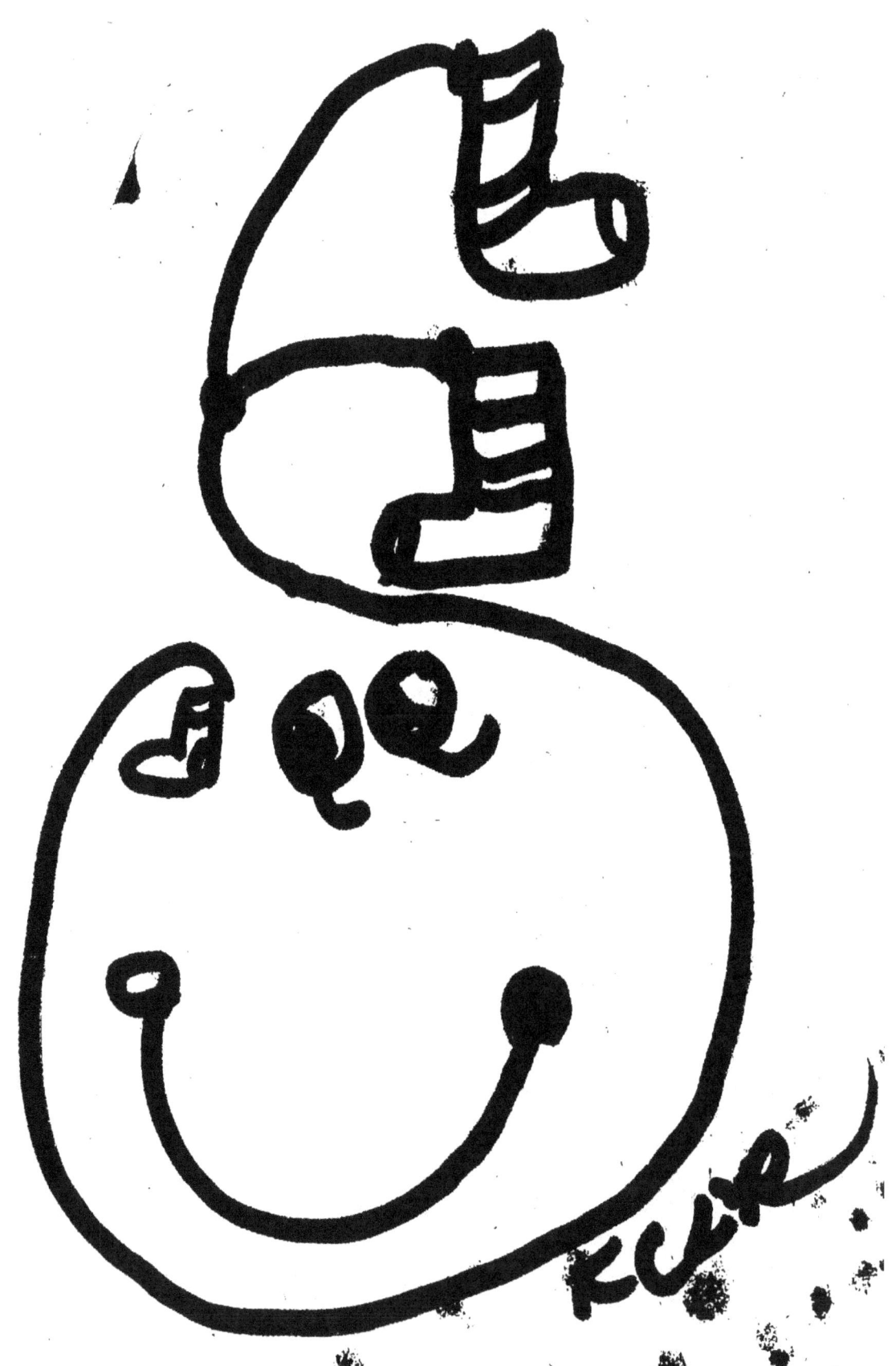

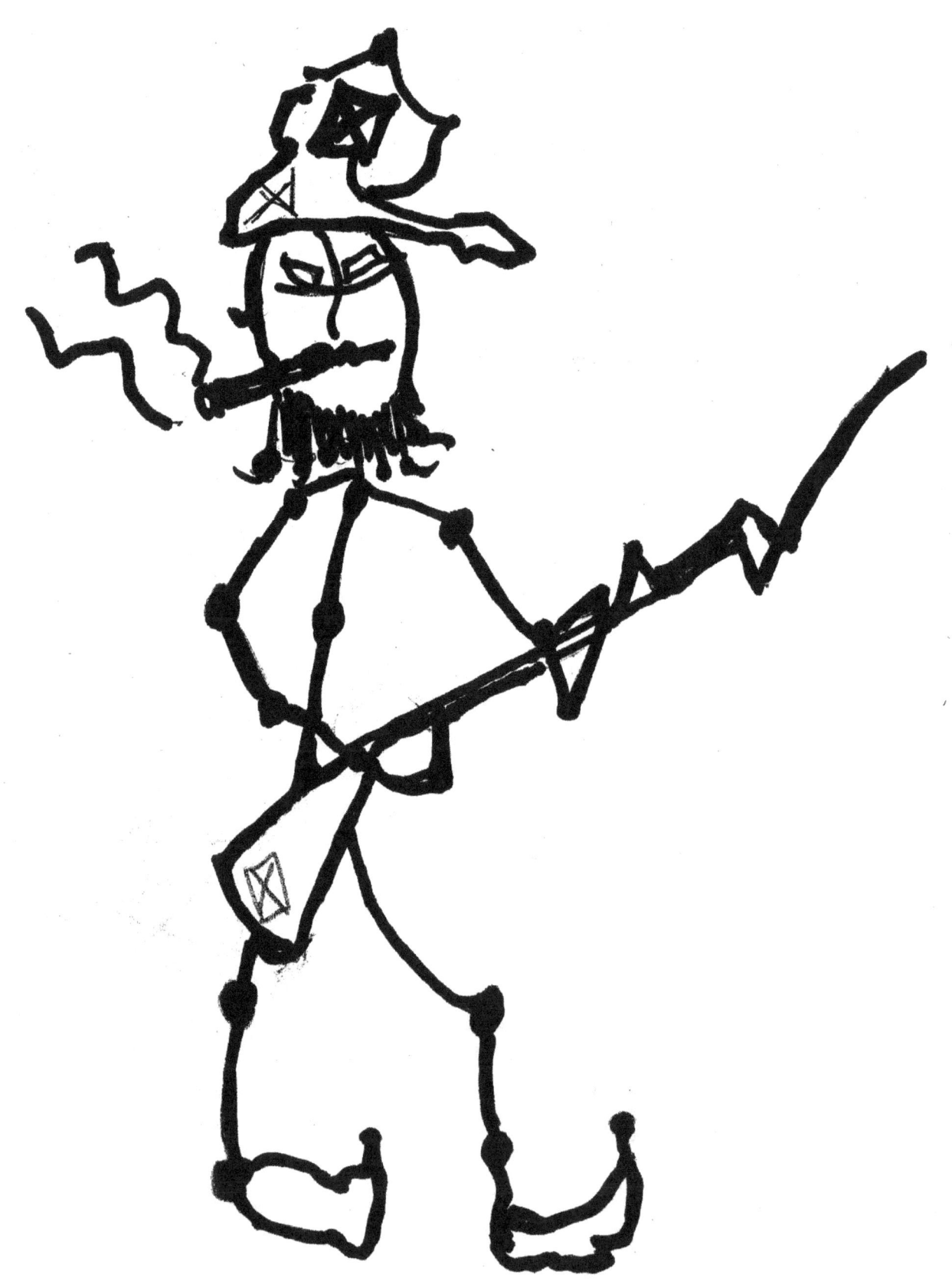

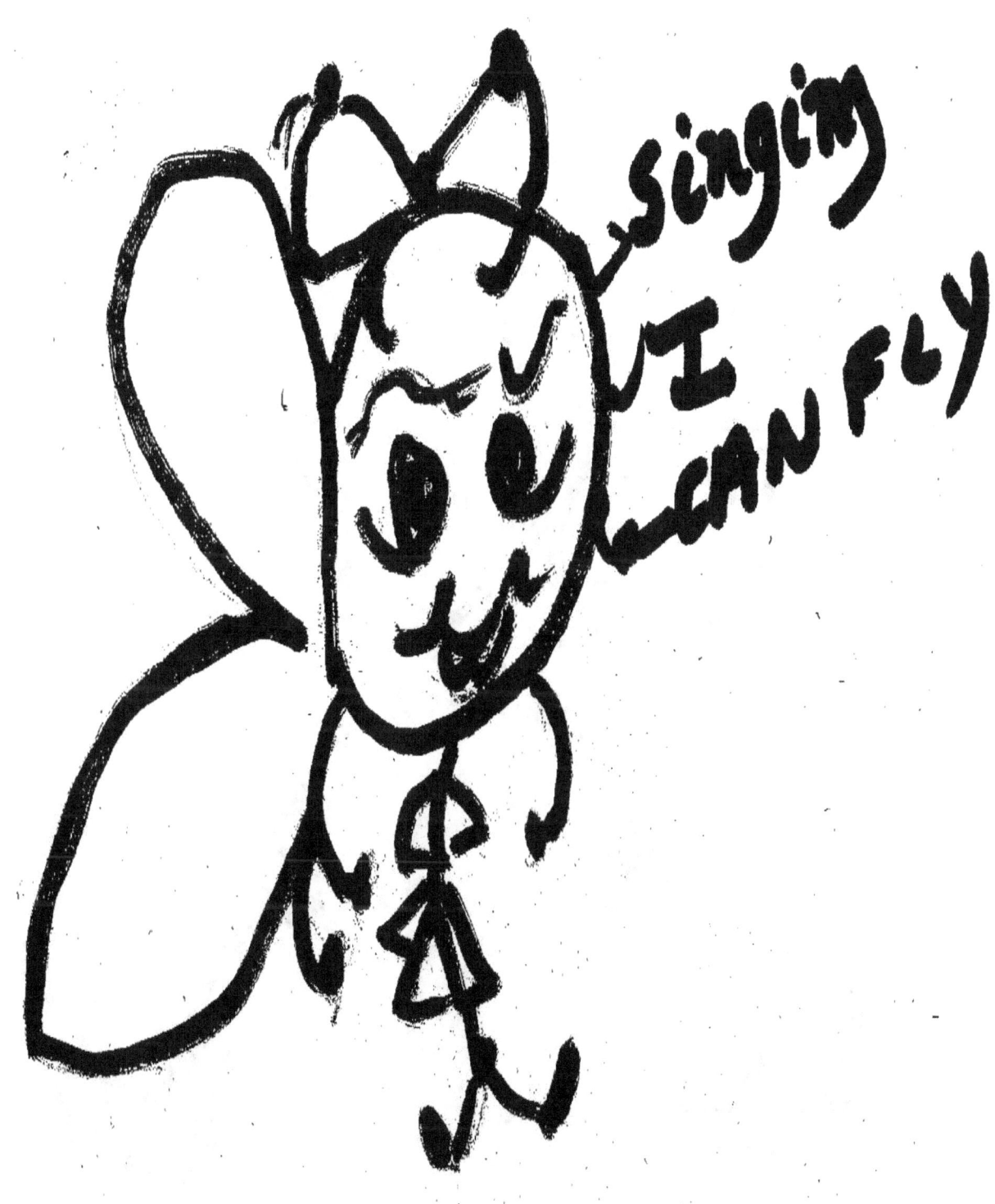

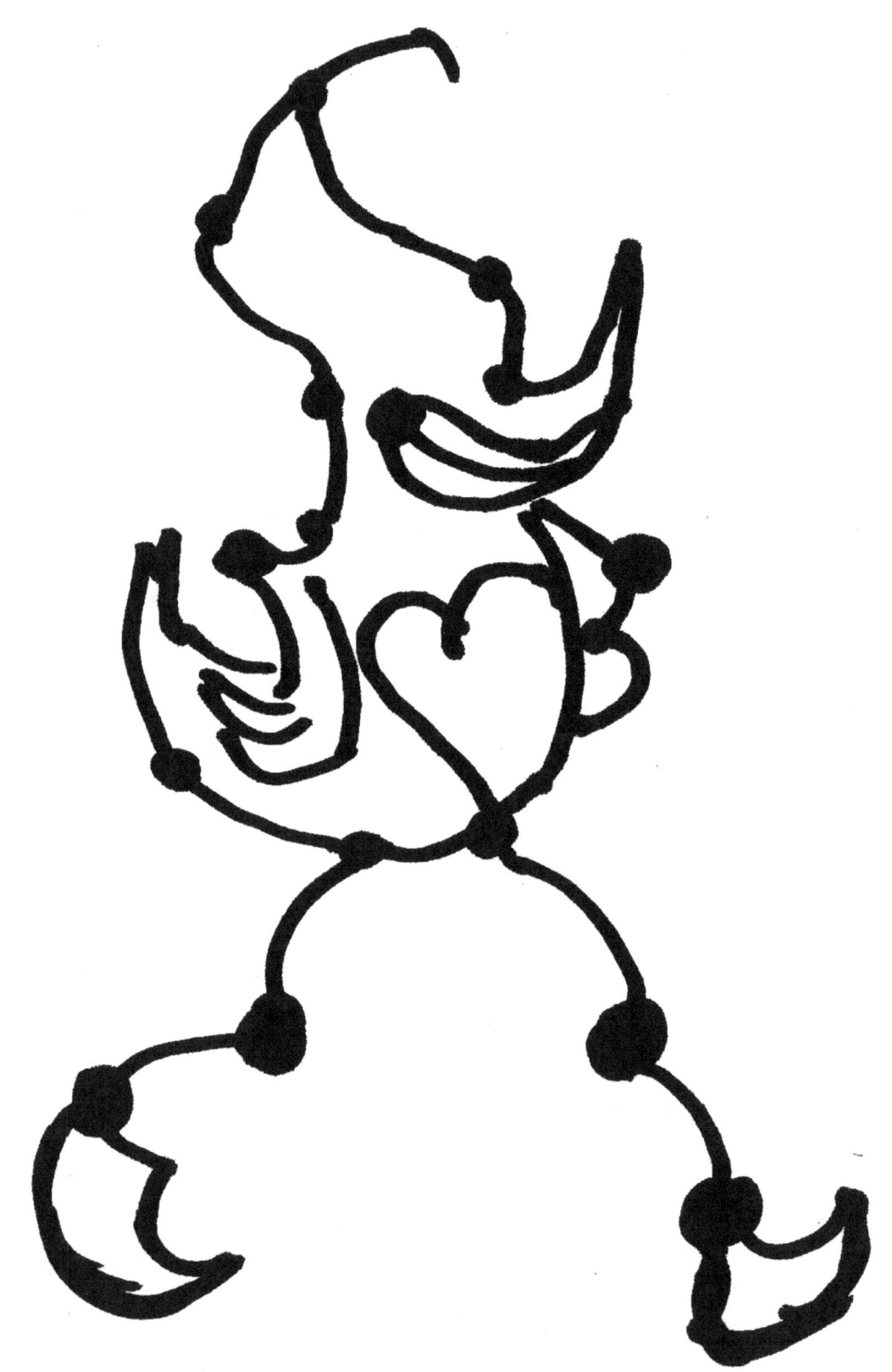

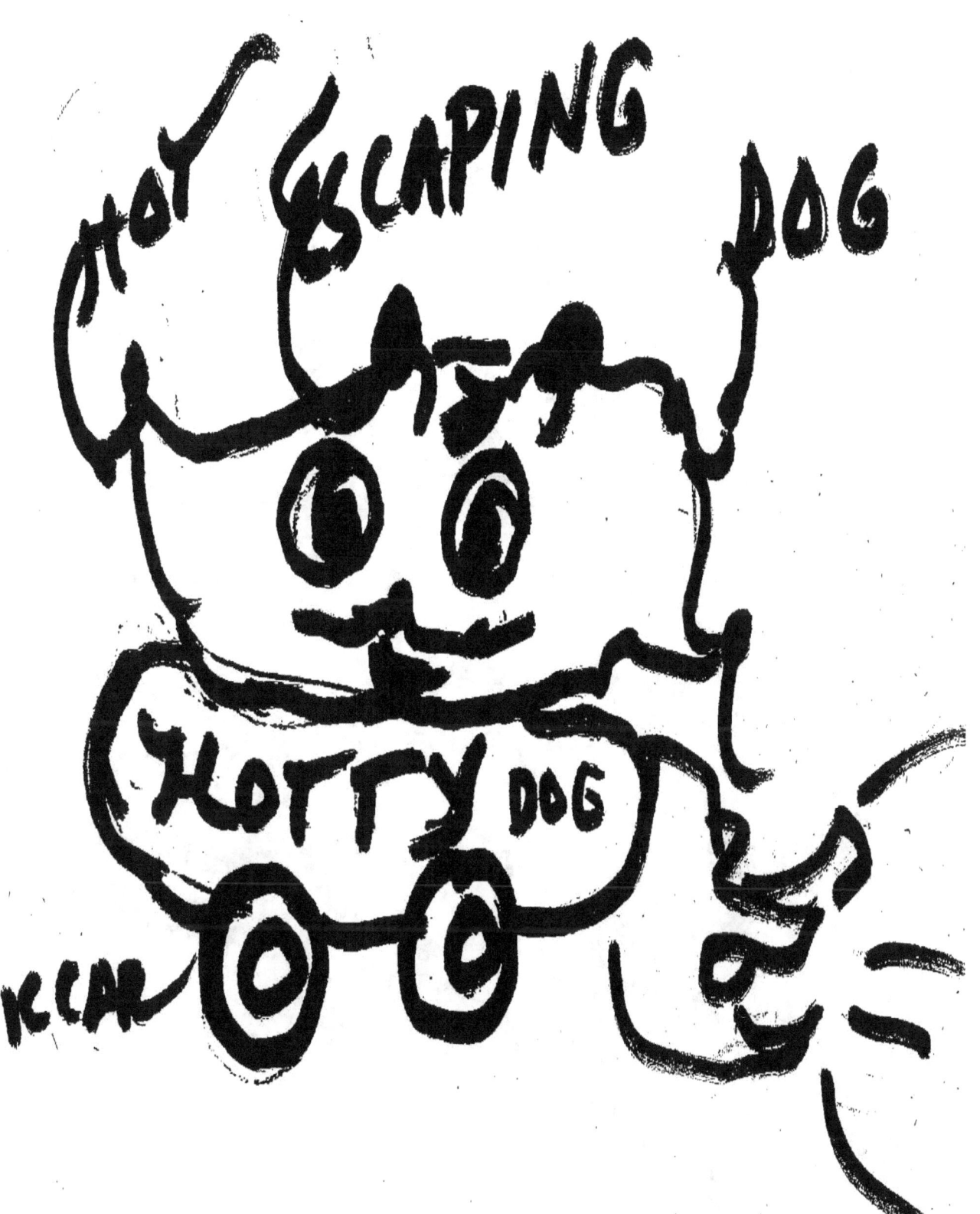

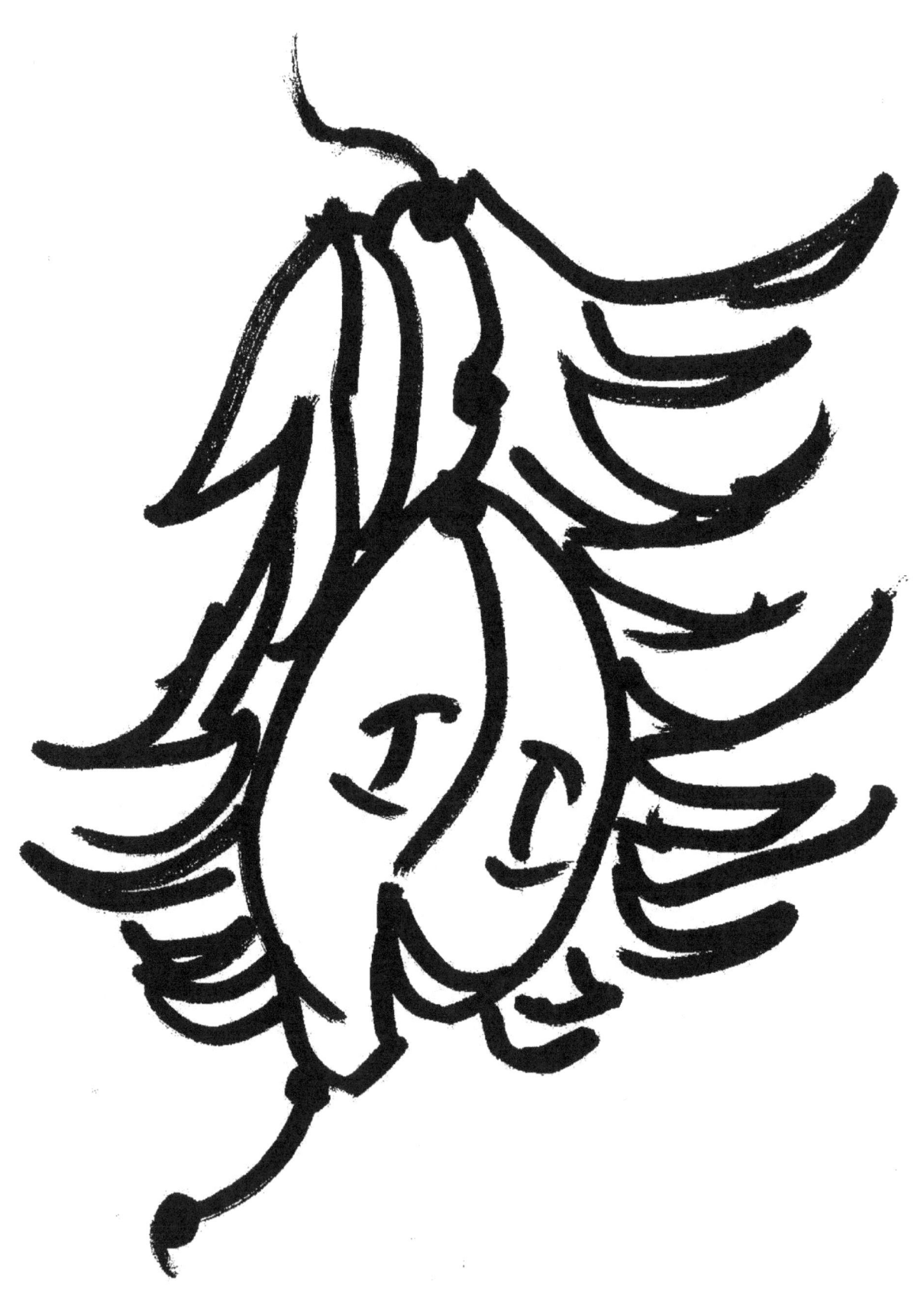

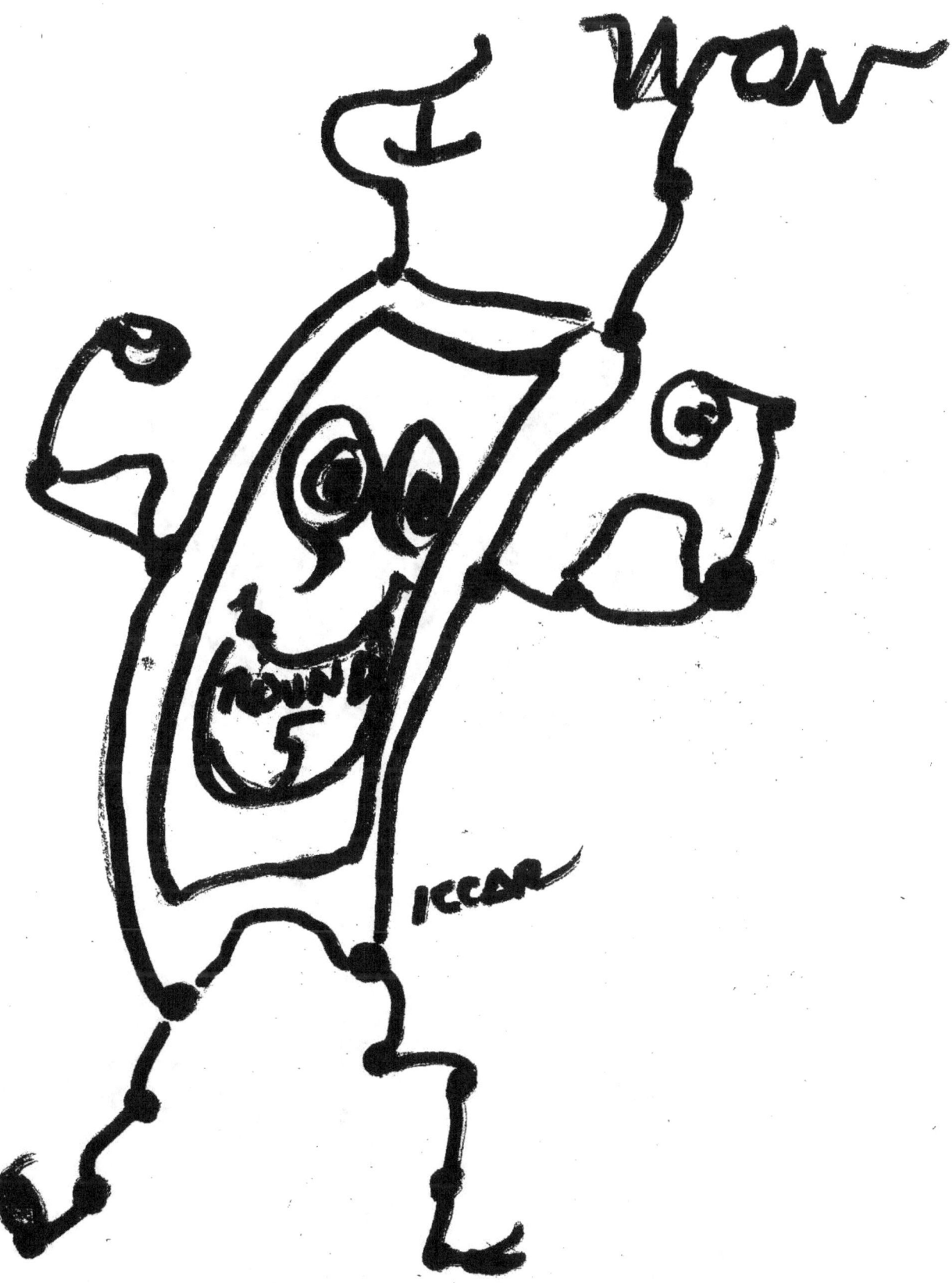

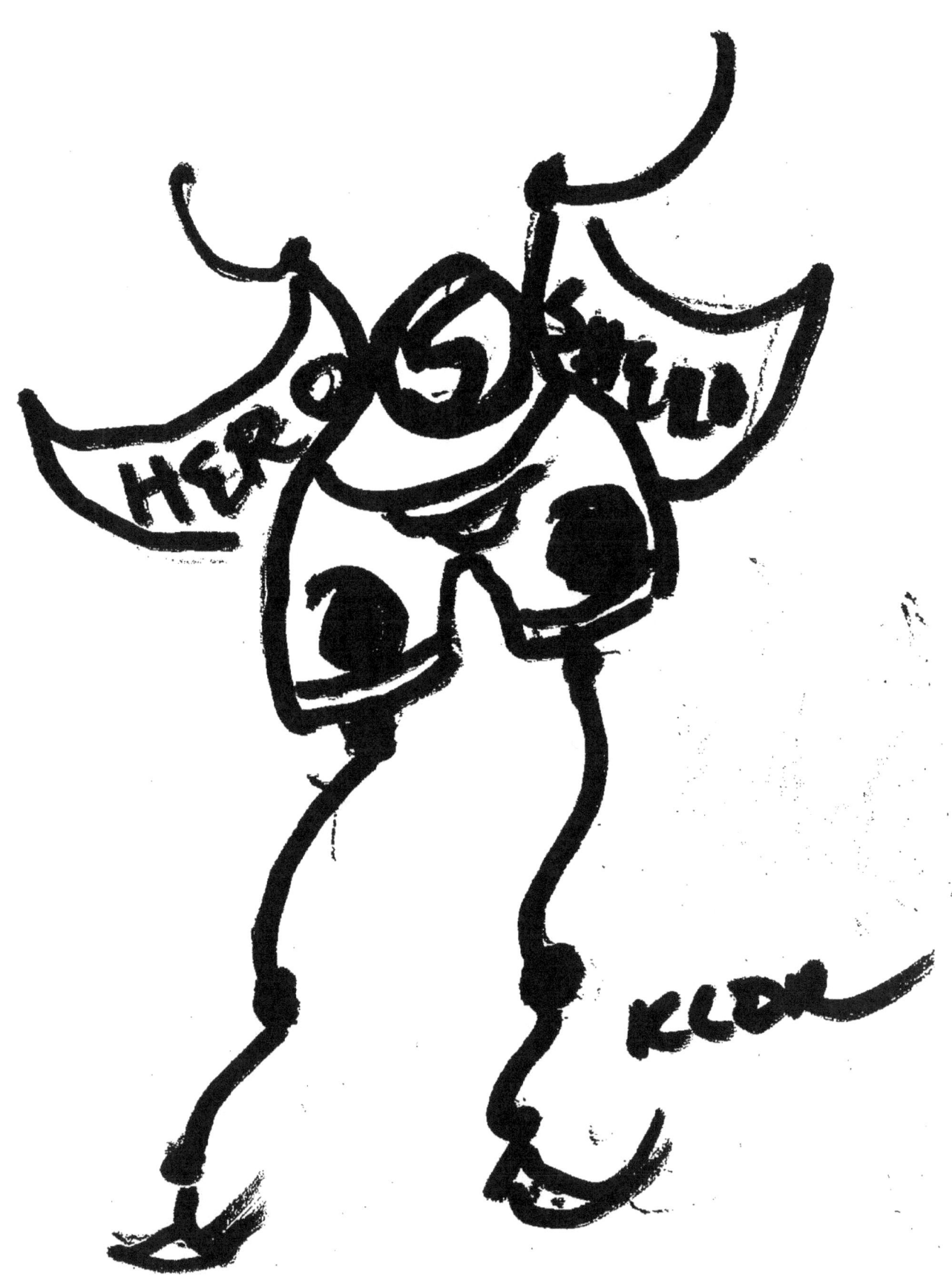

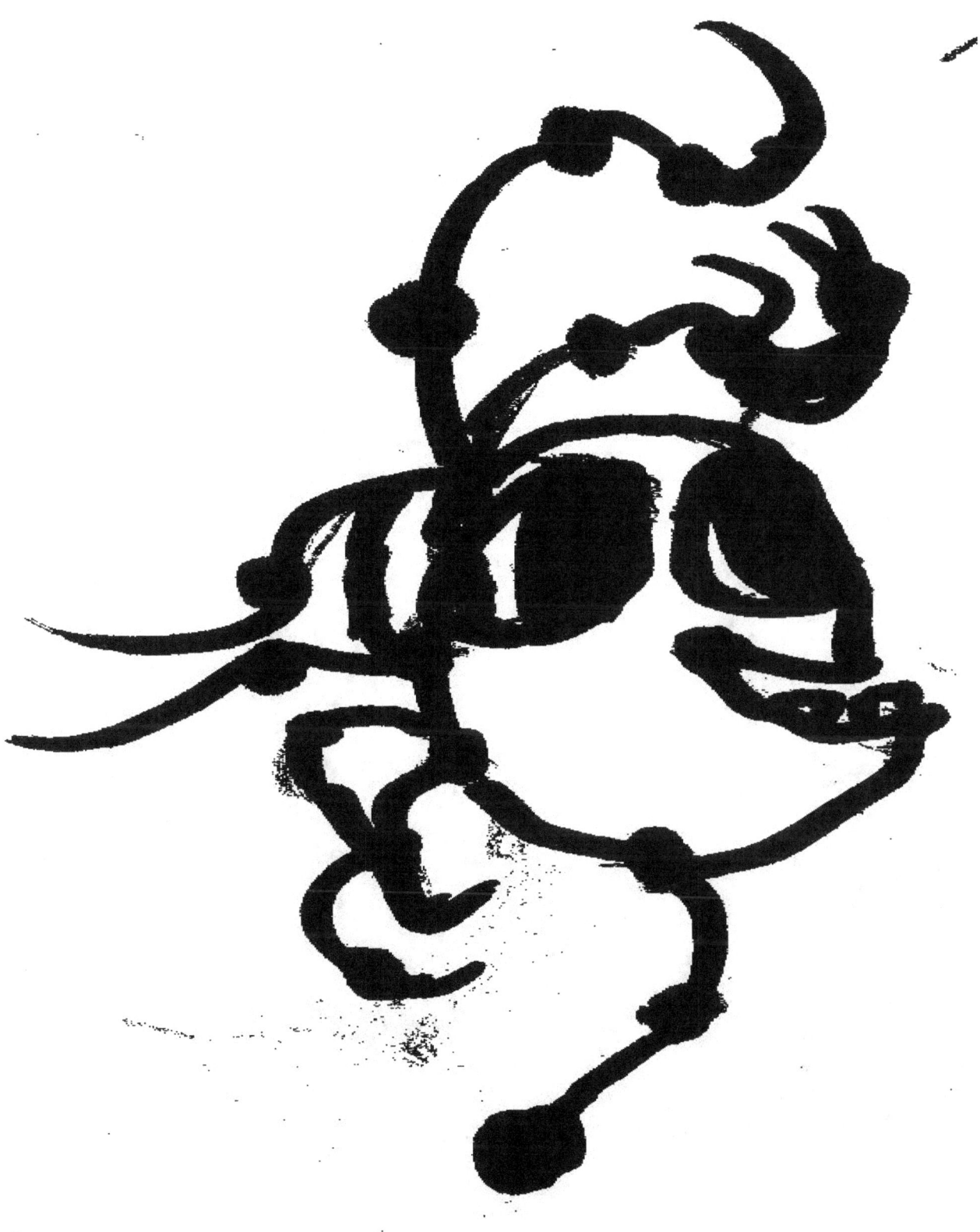

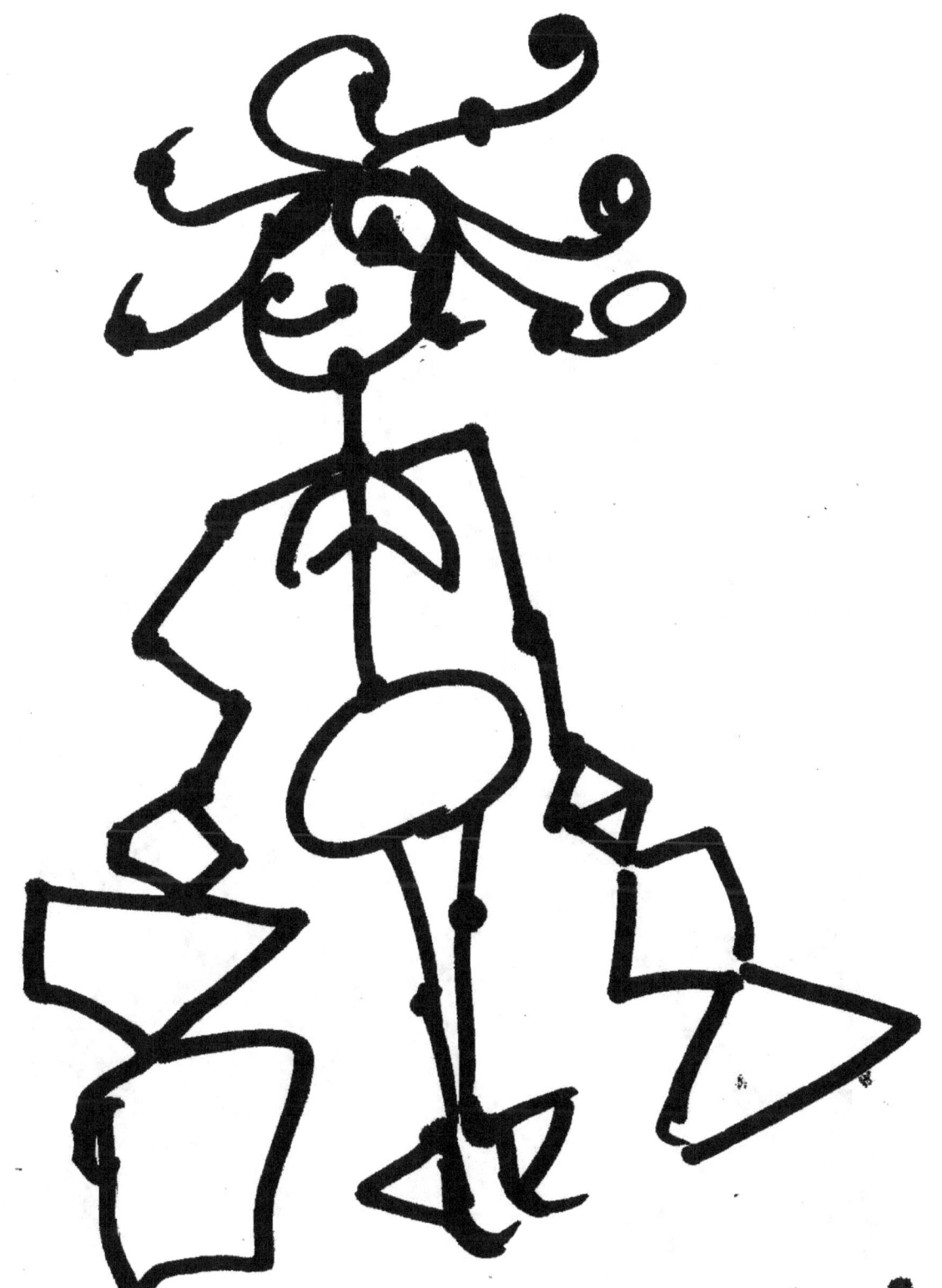

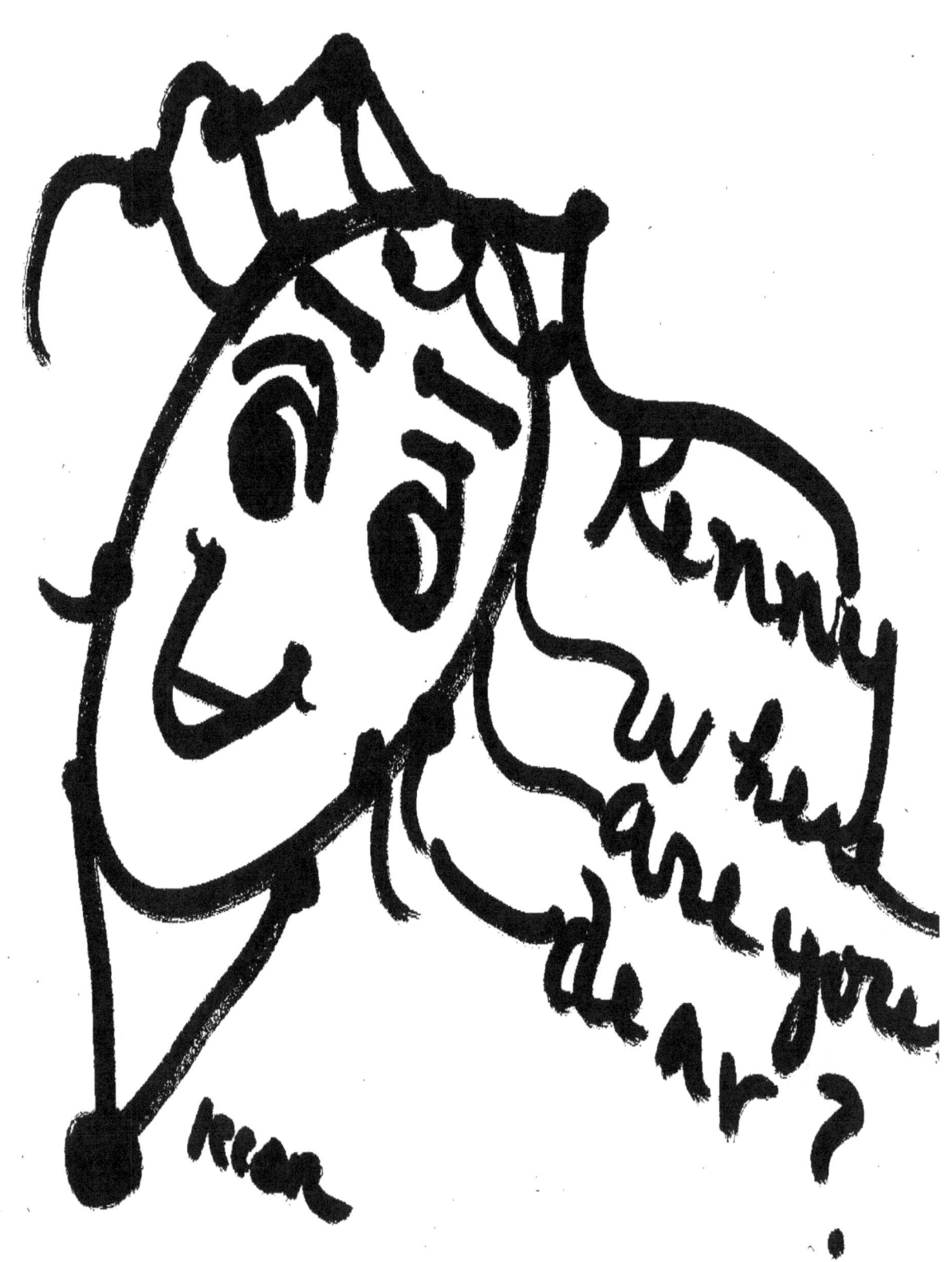

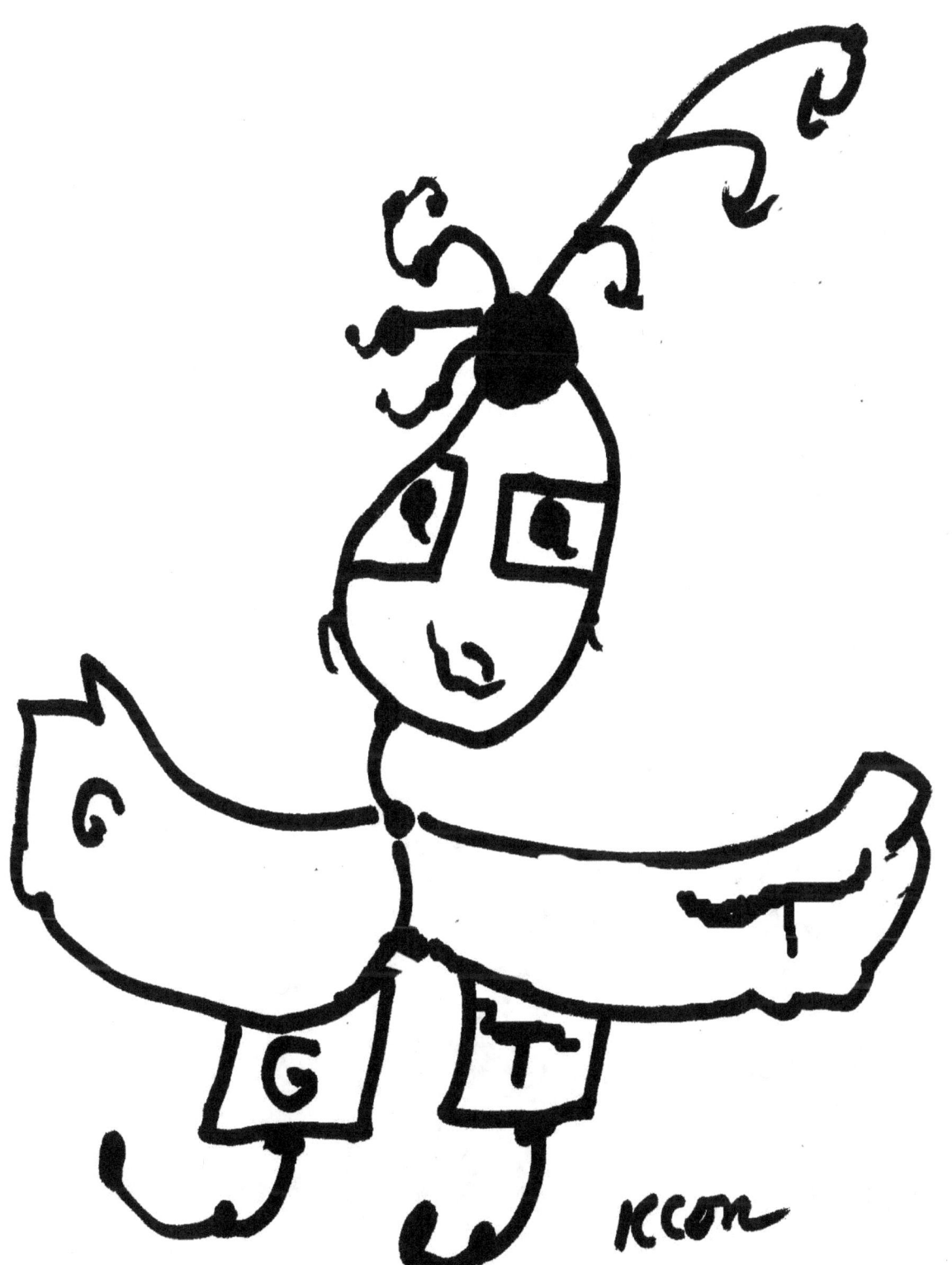

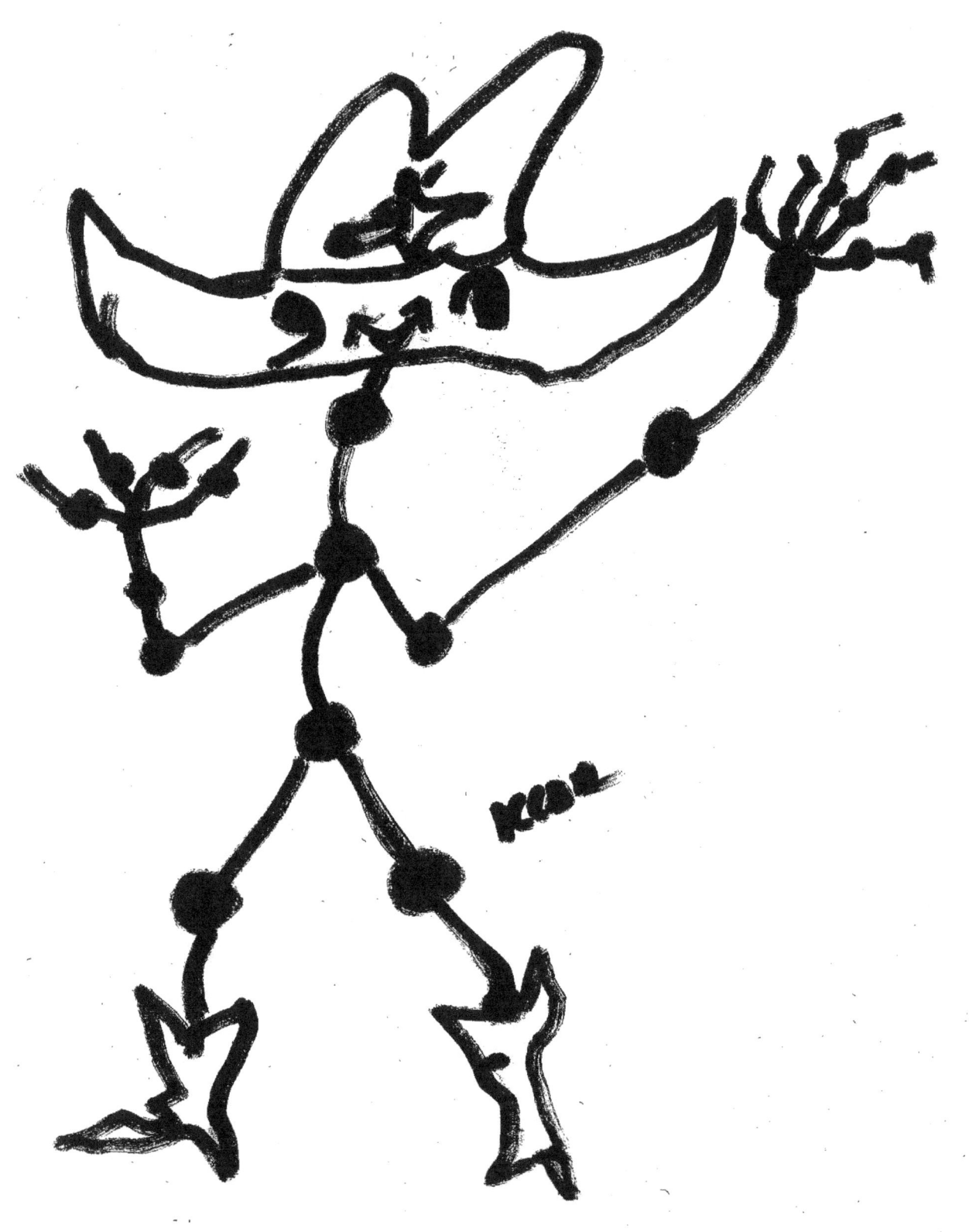

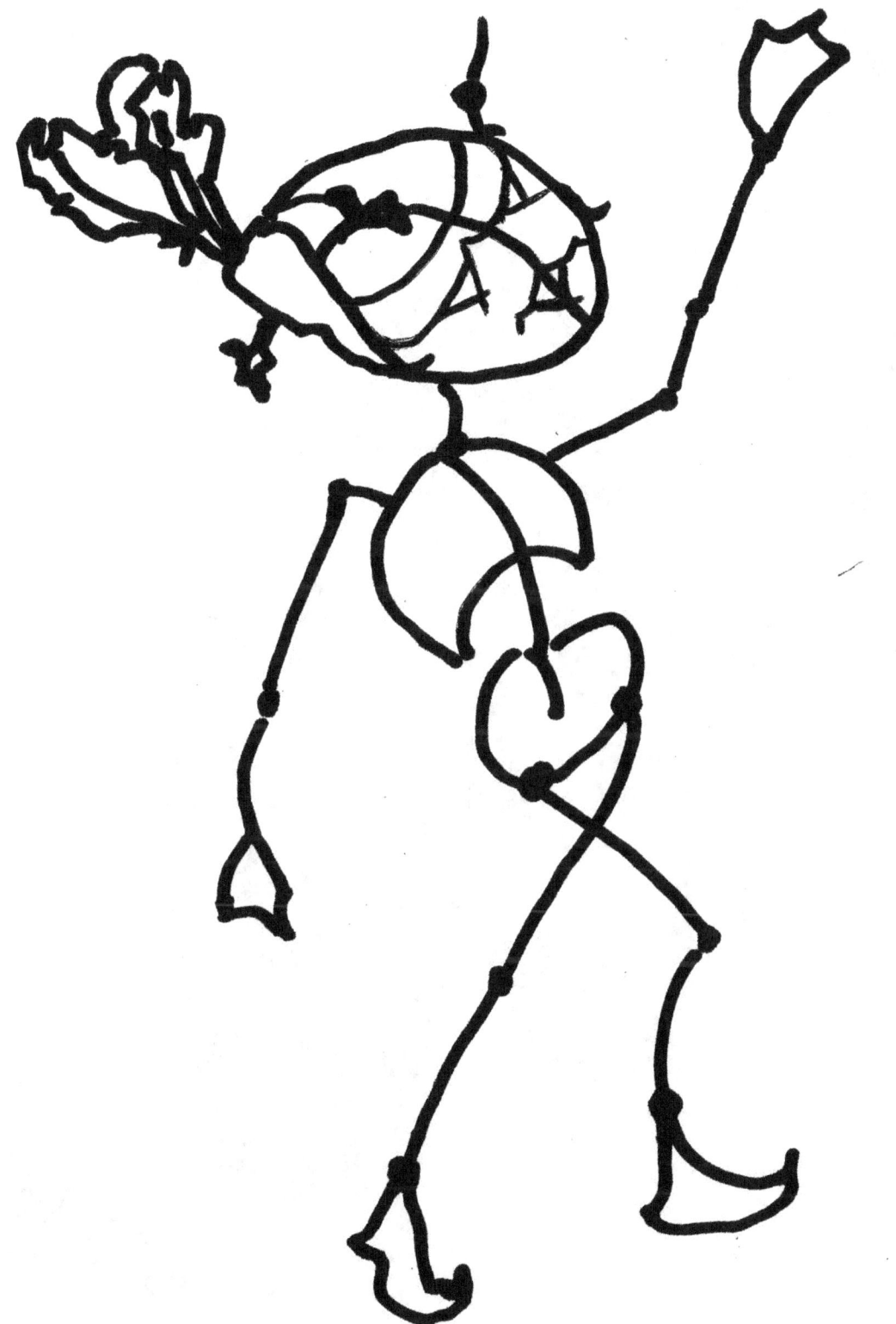

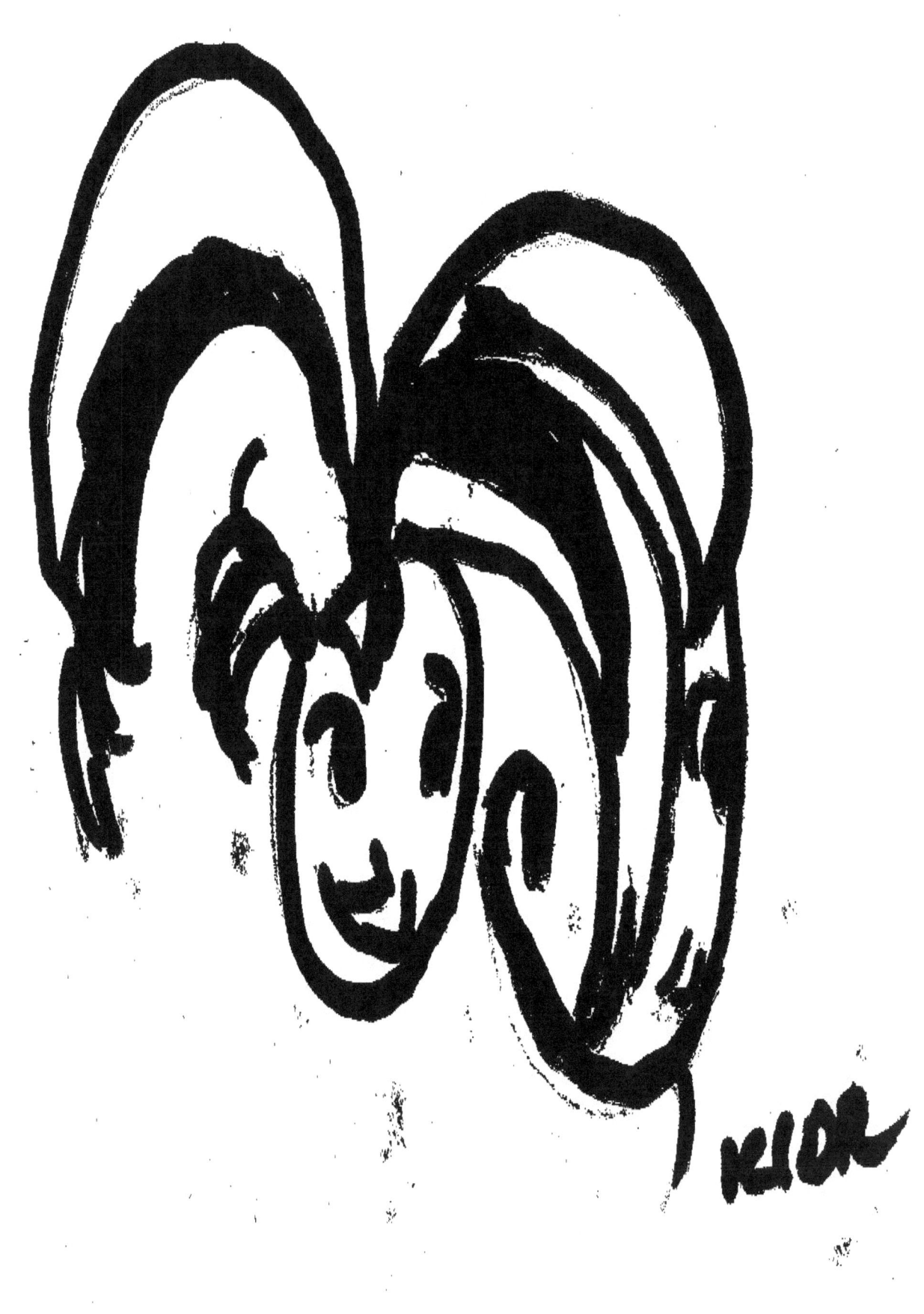

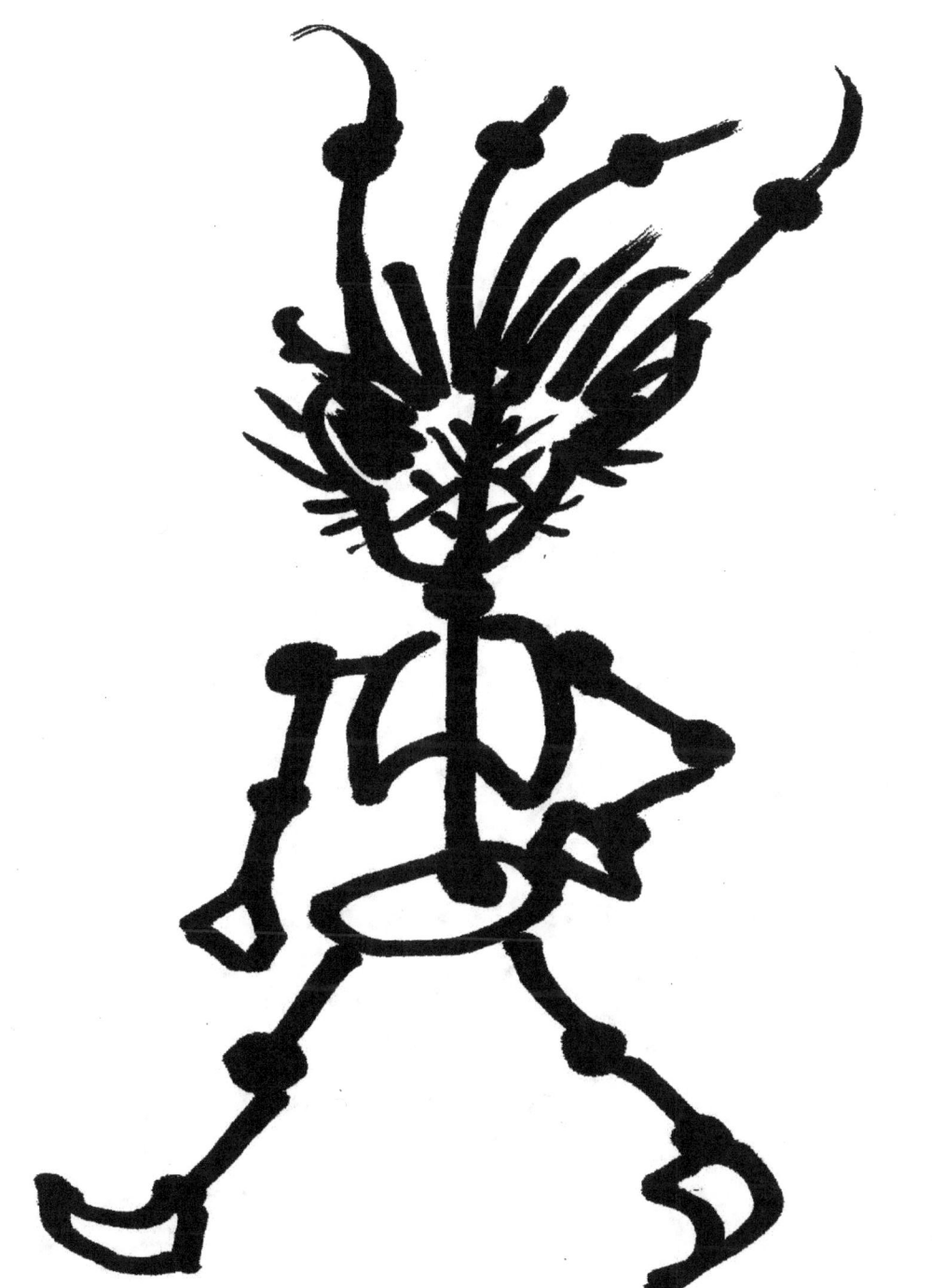

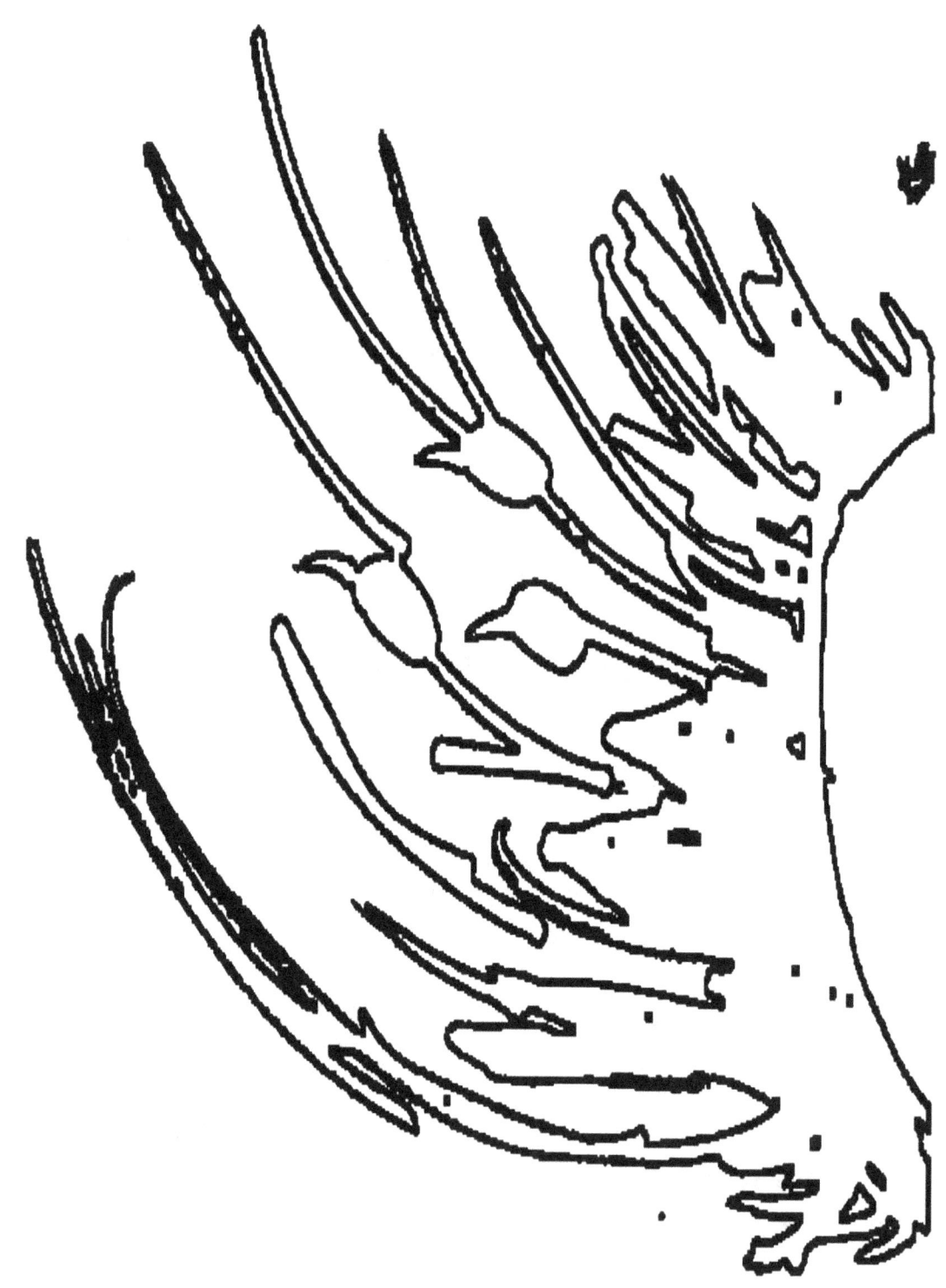

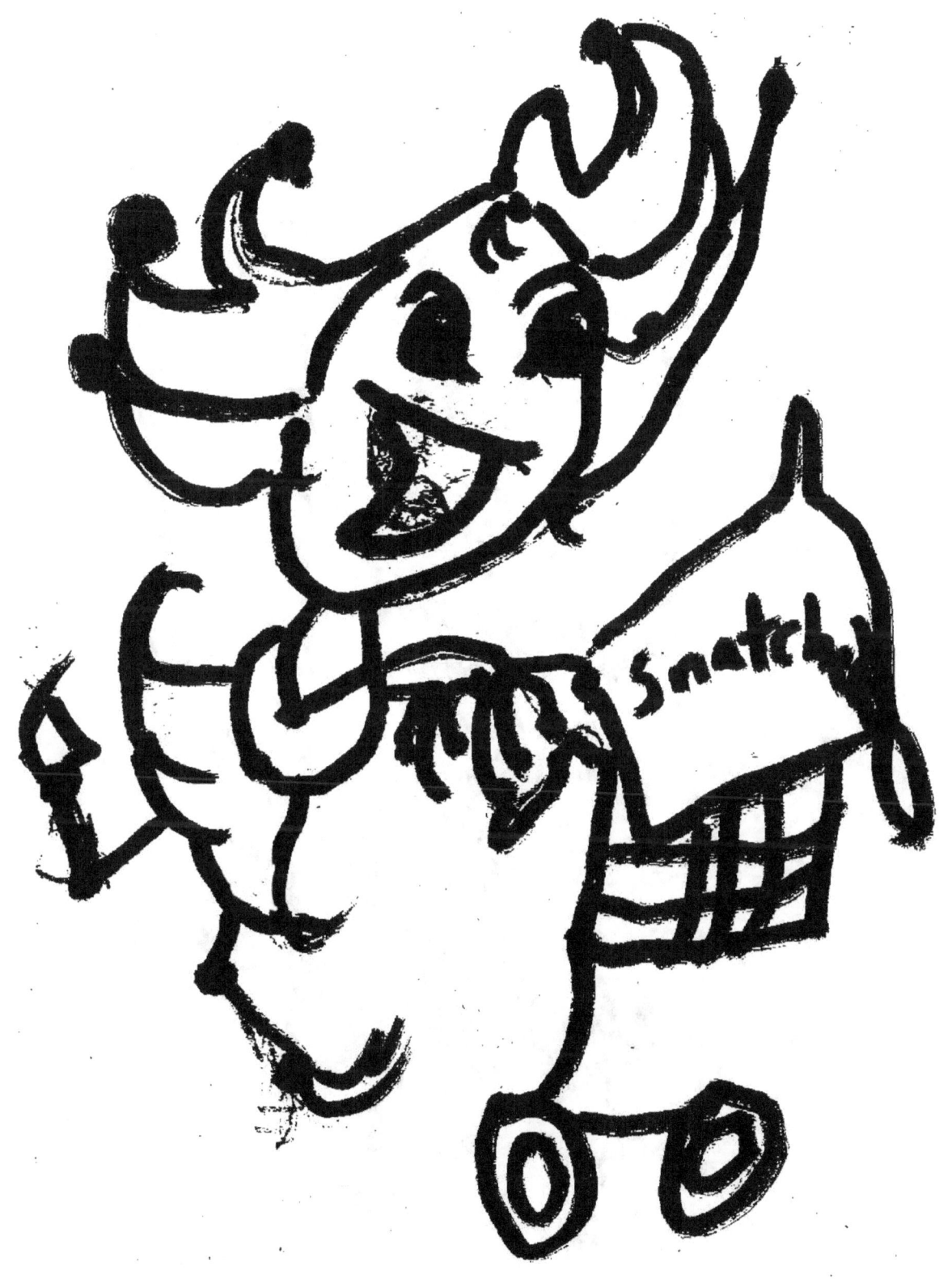

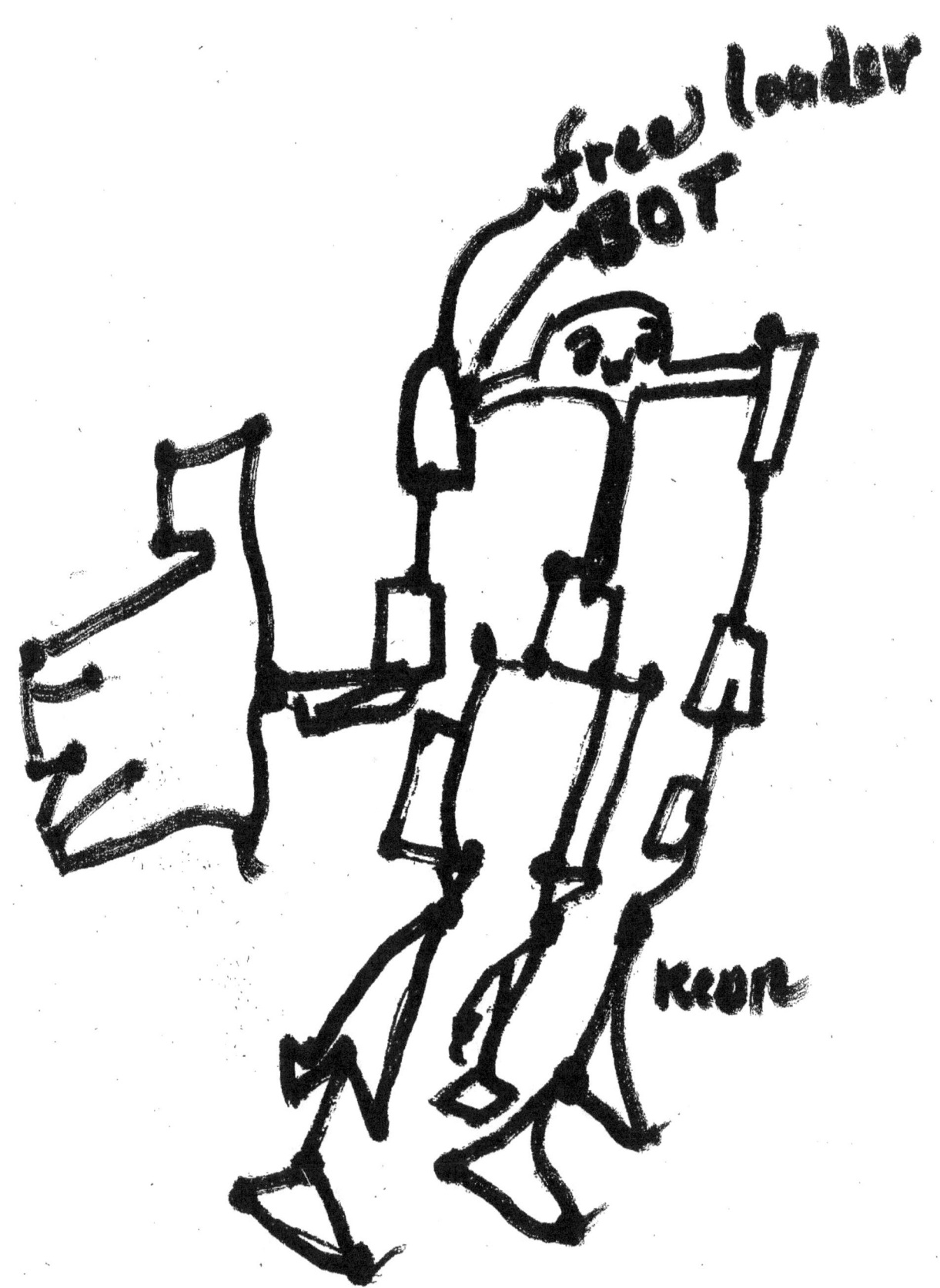

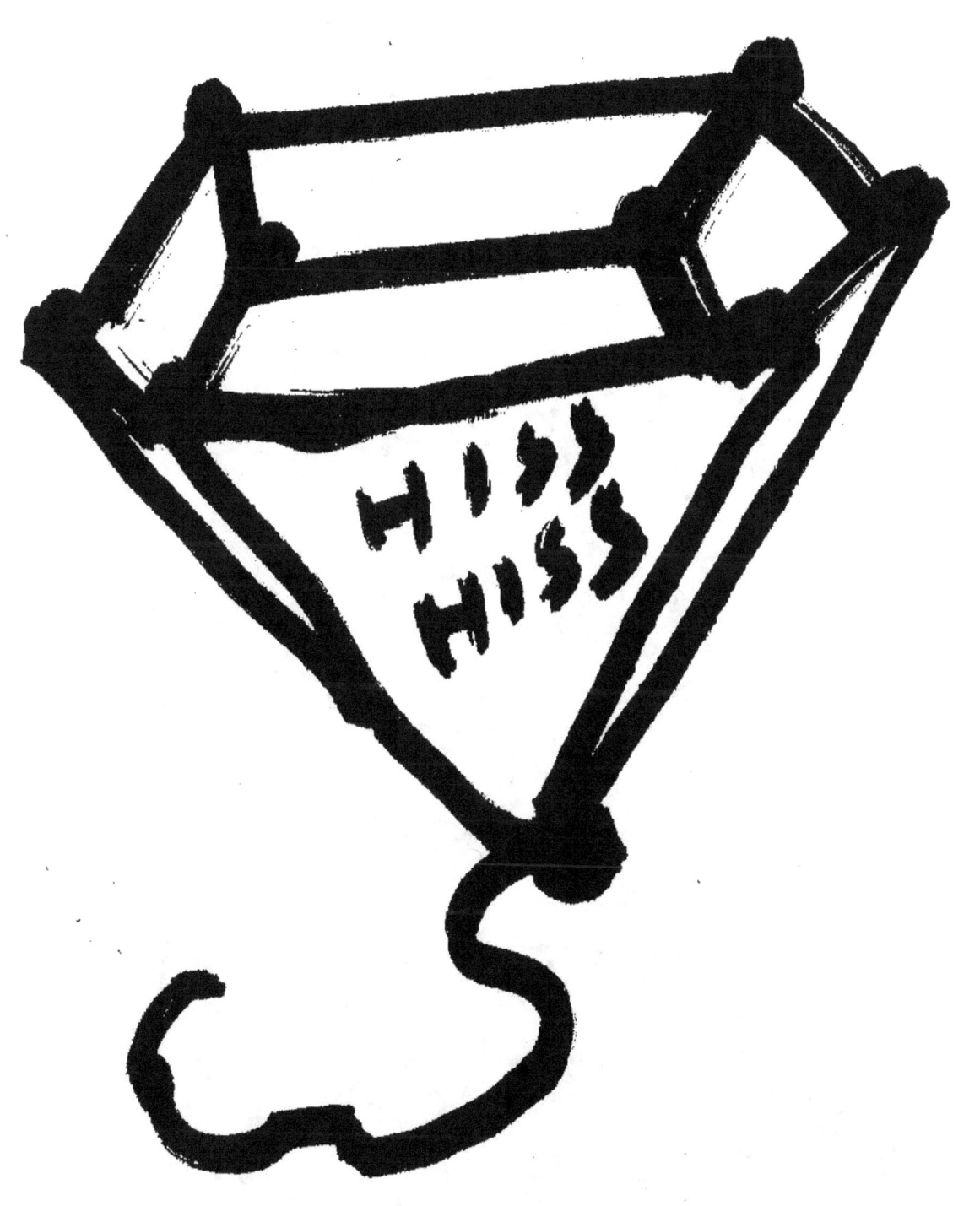

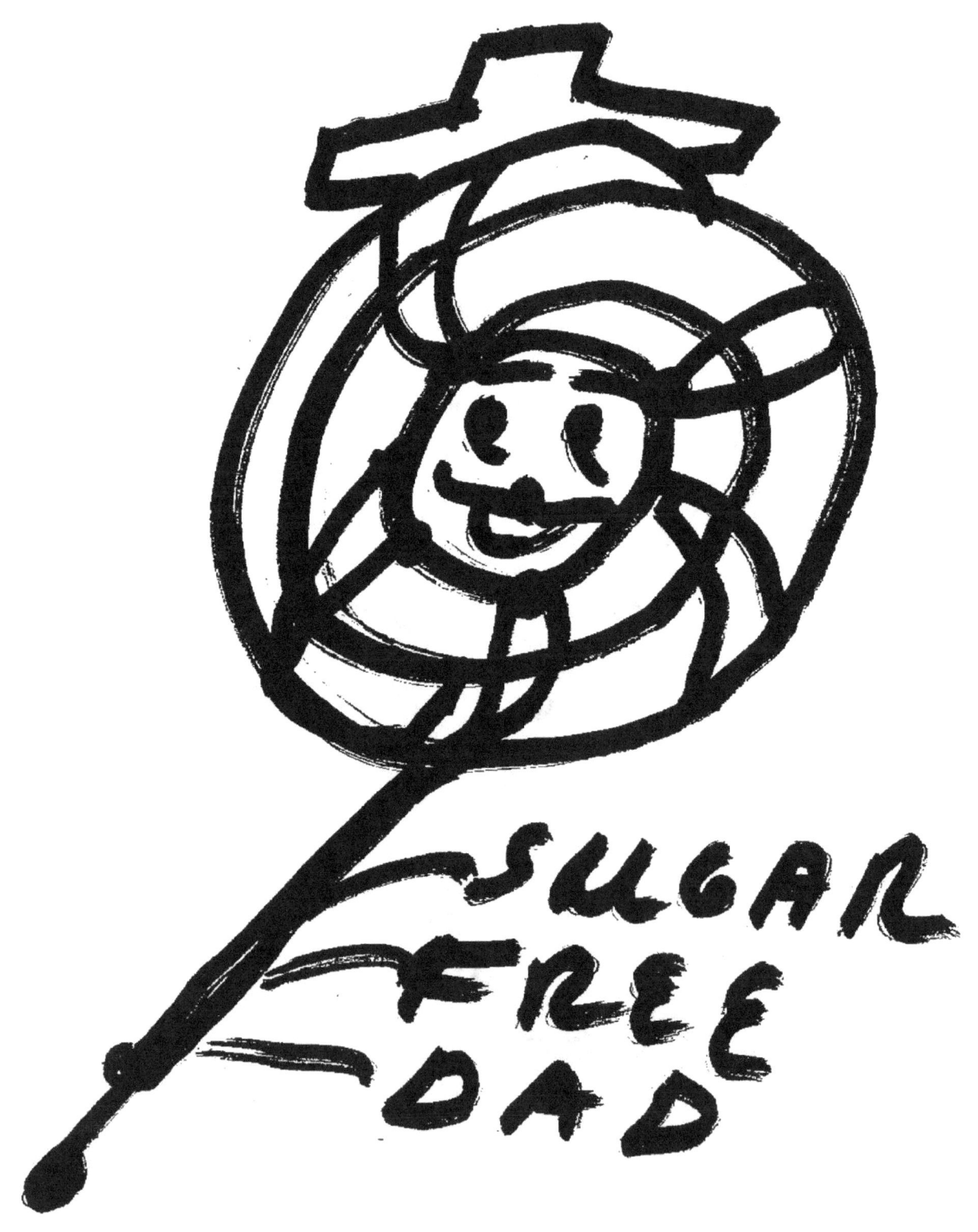

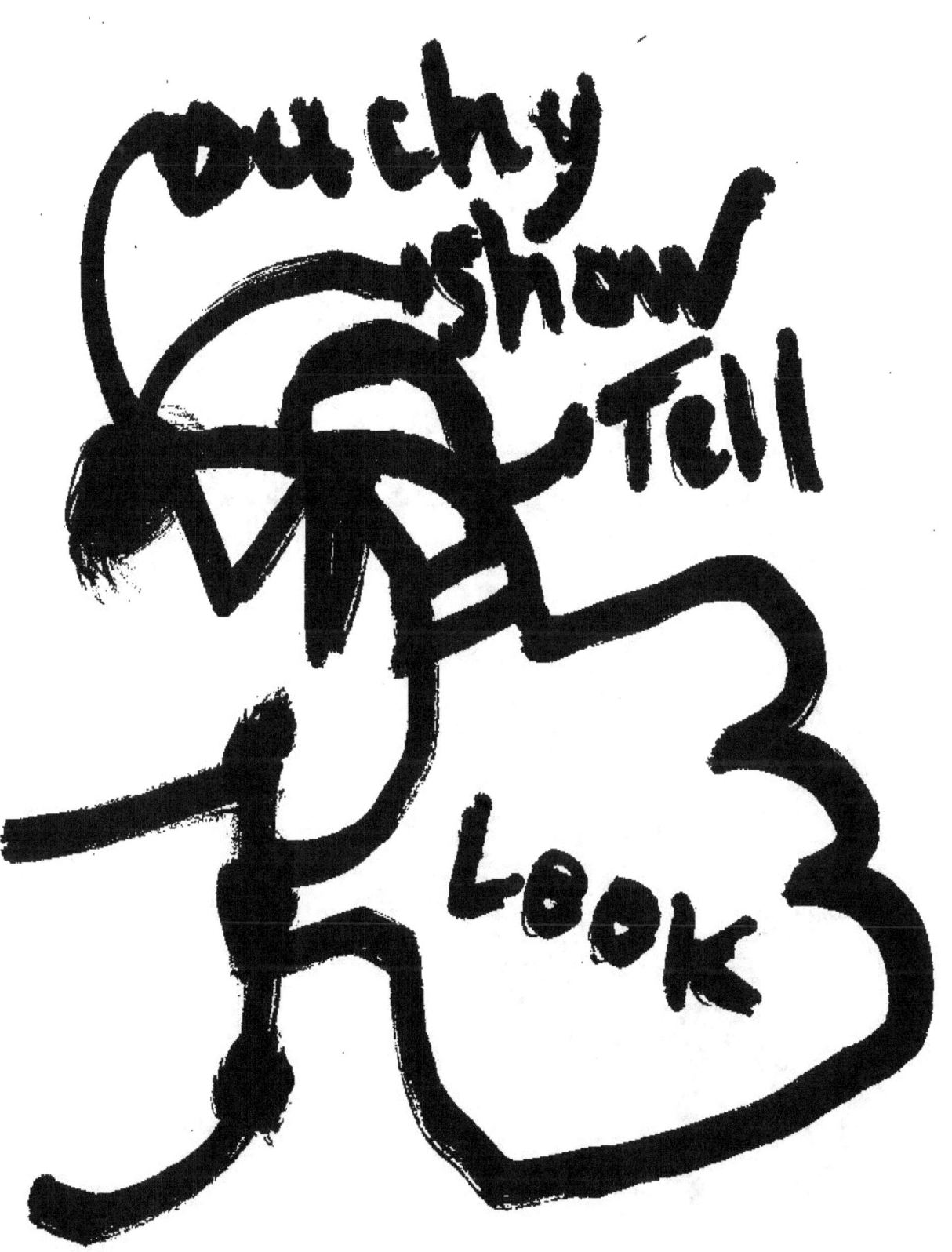

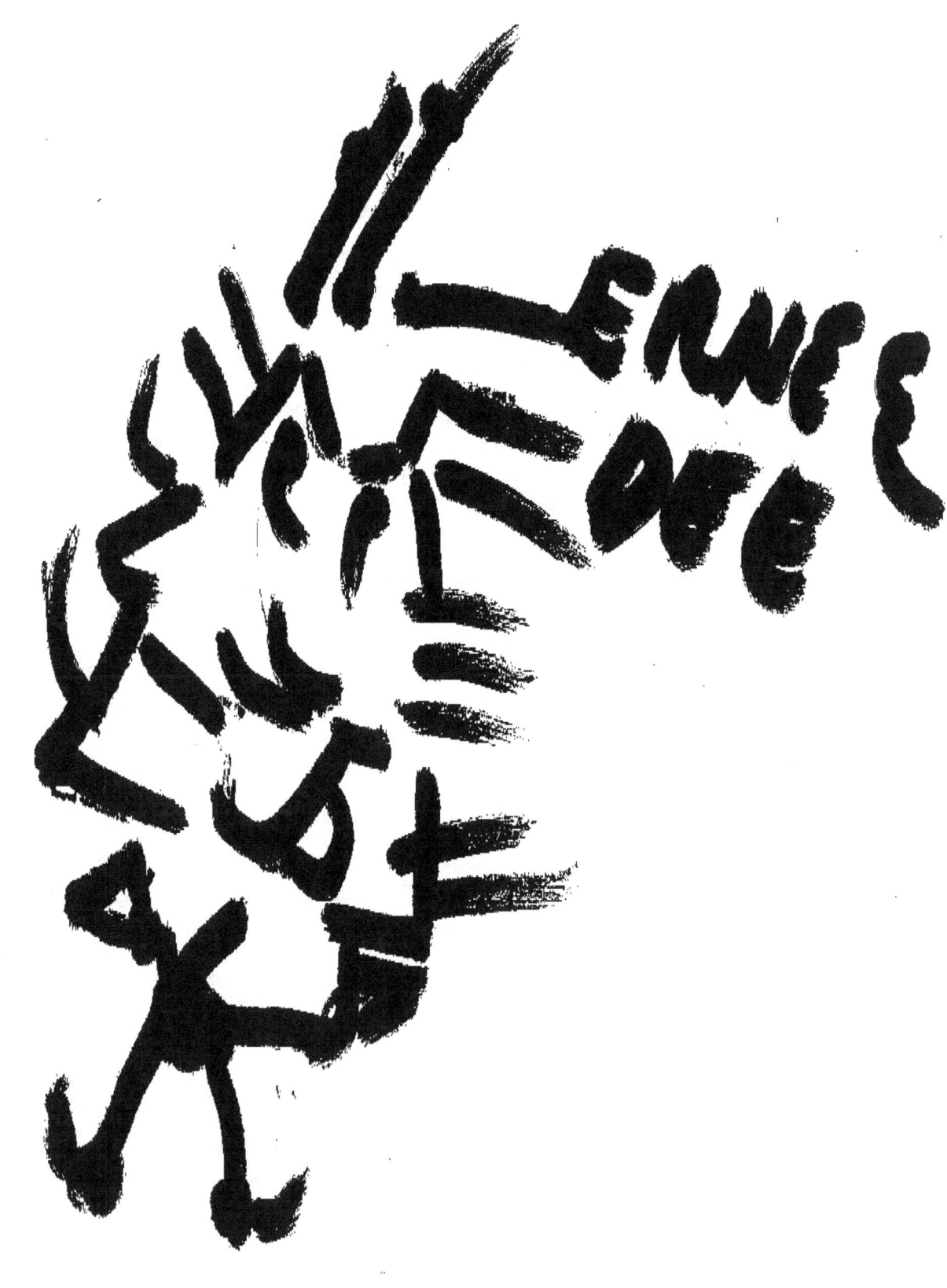

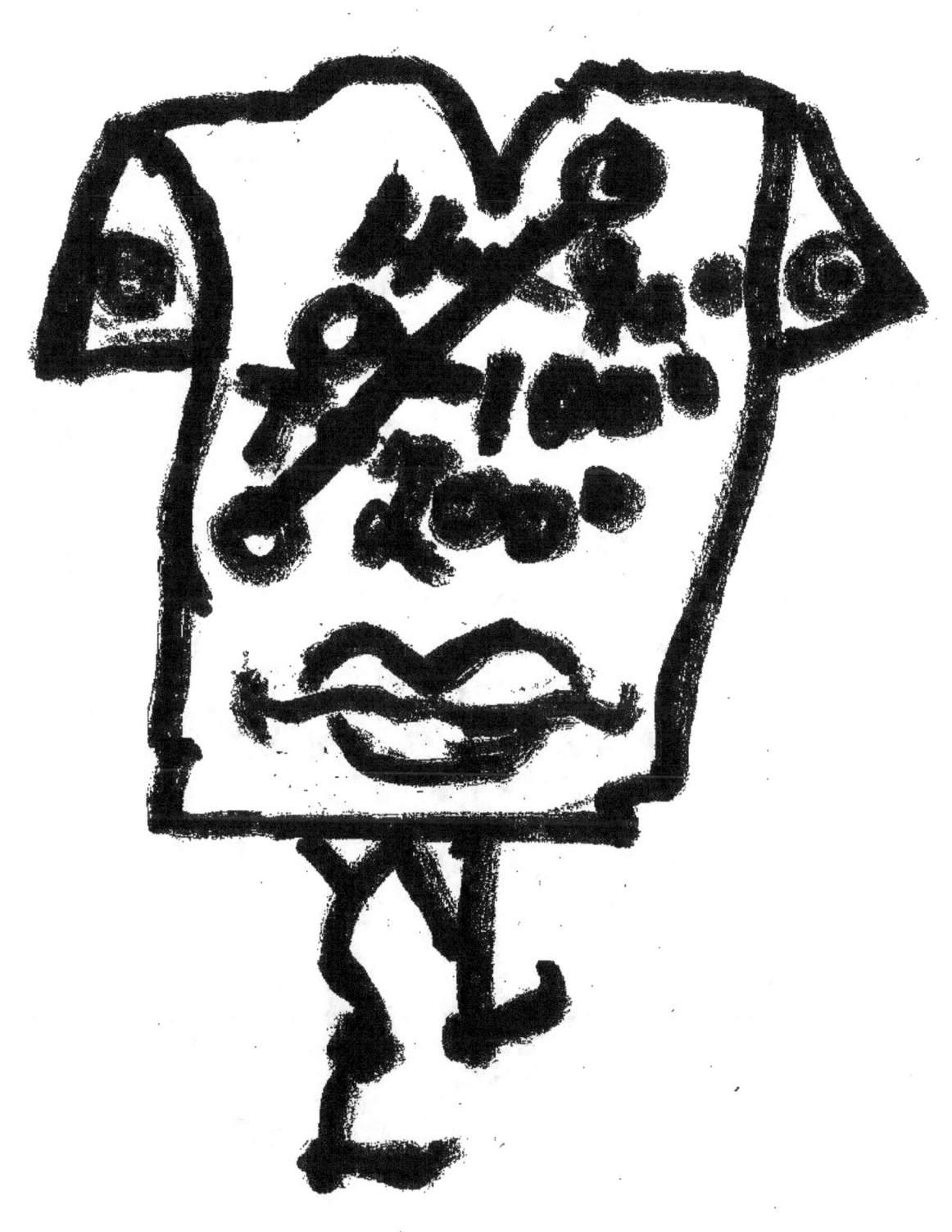

lamps

popsickles

marbles

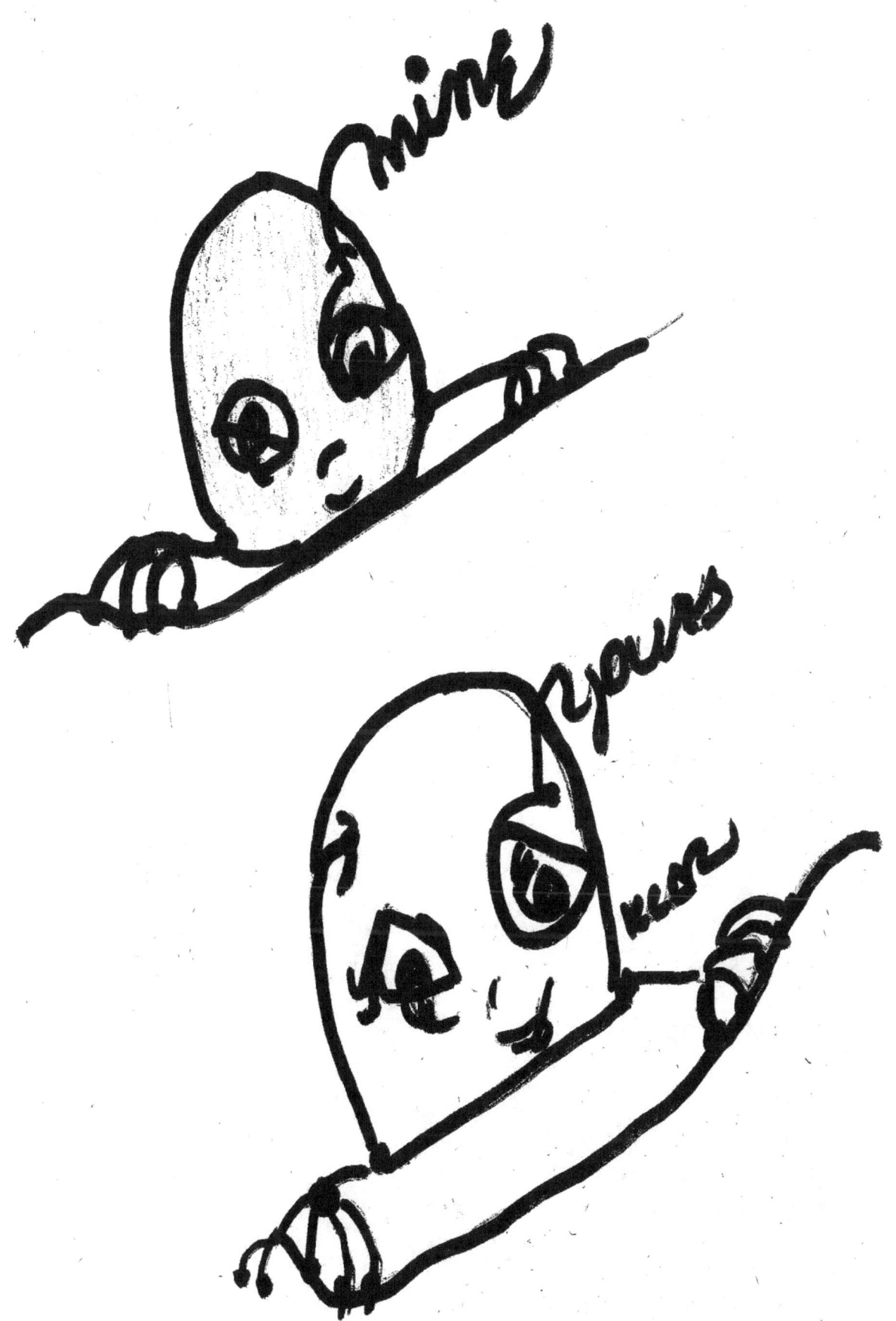

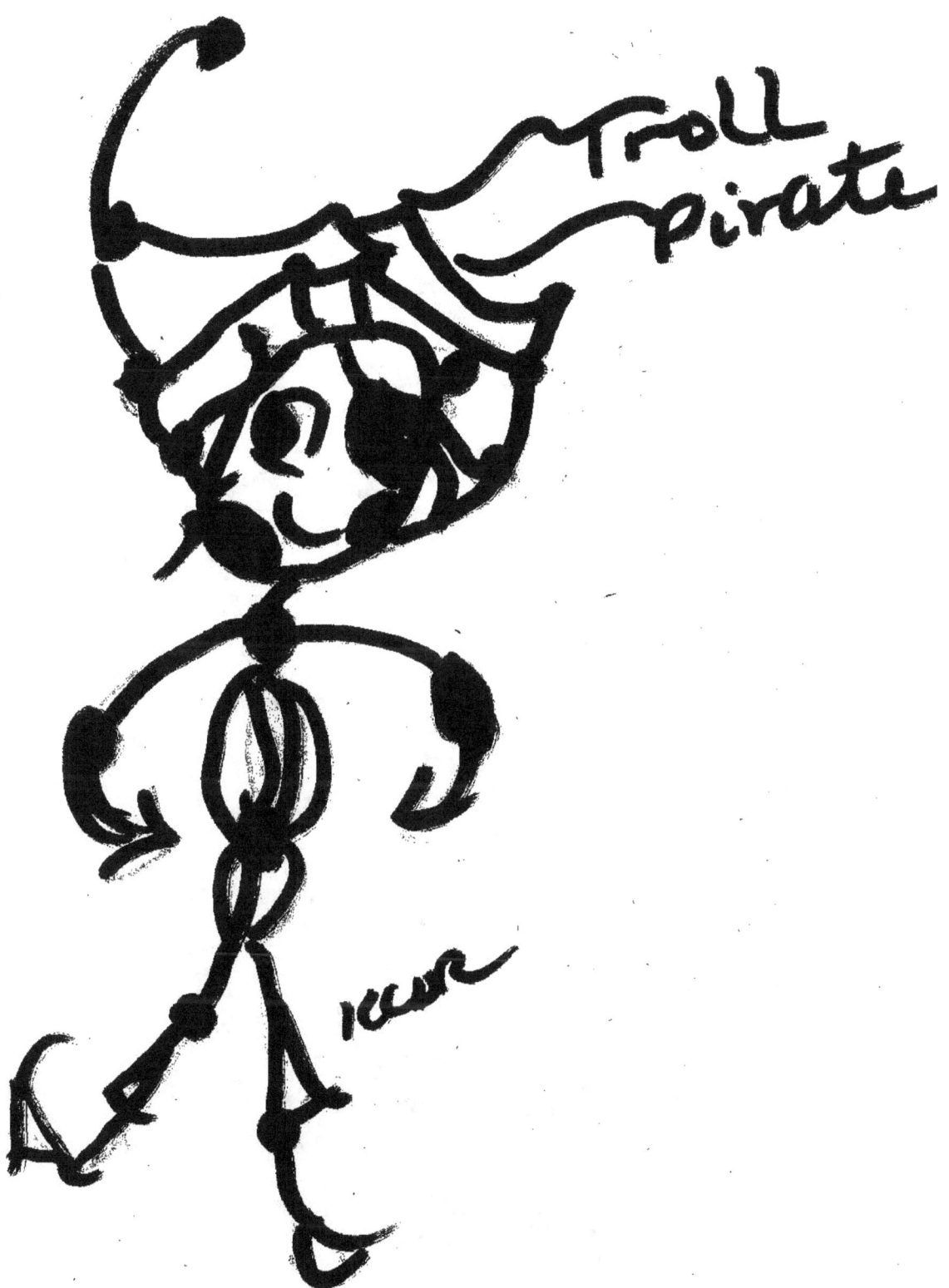

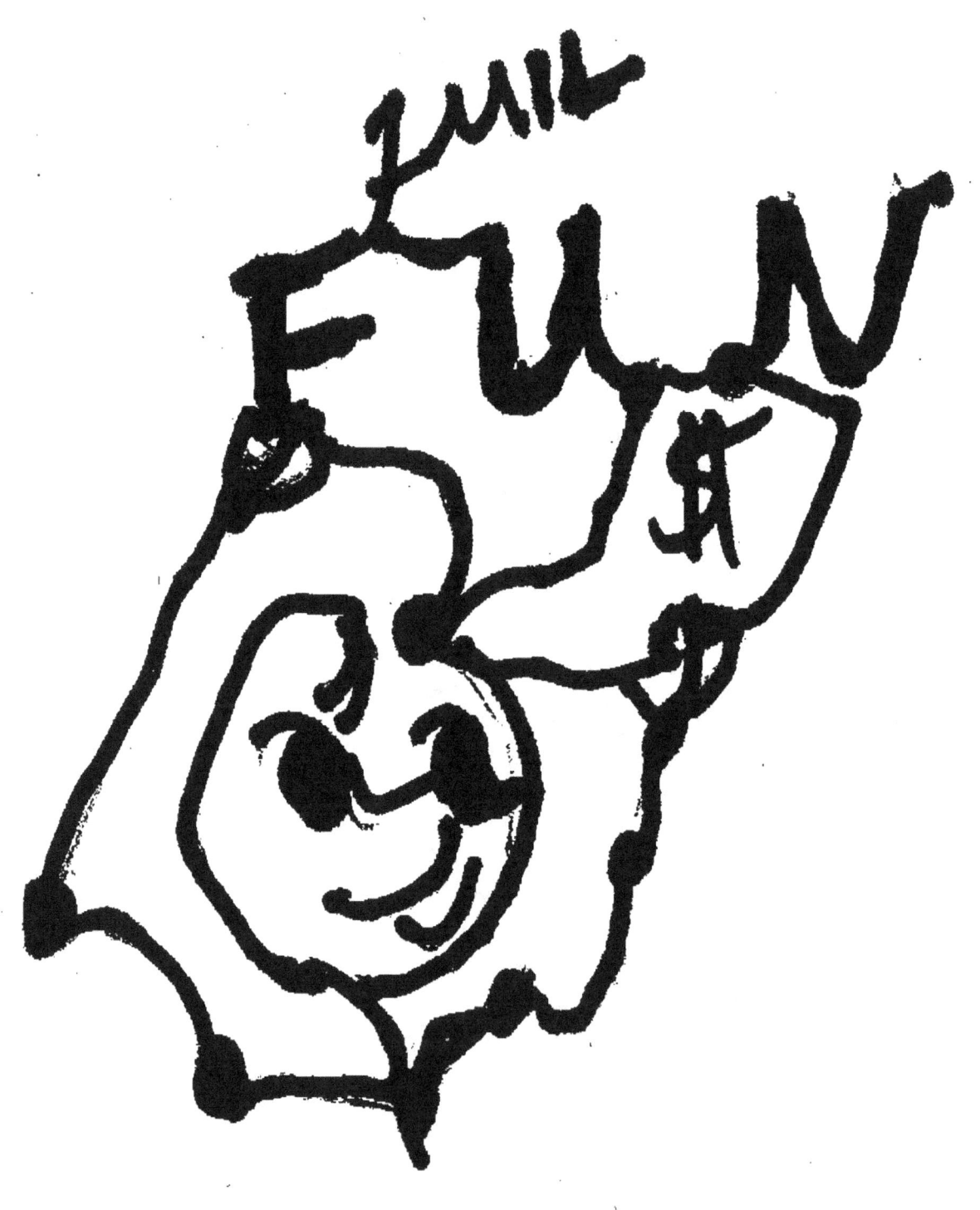

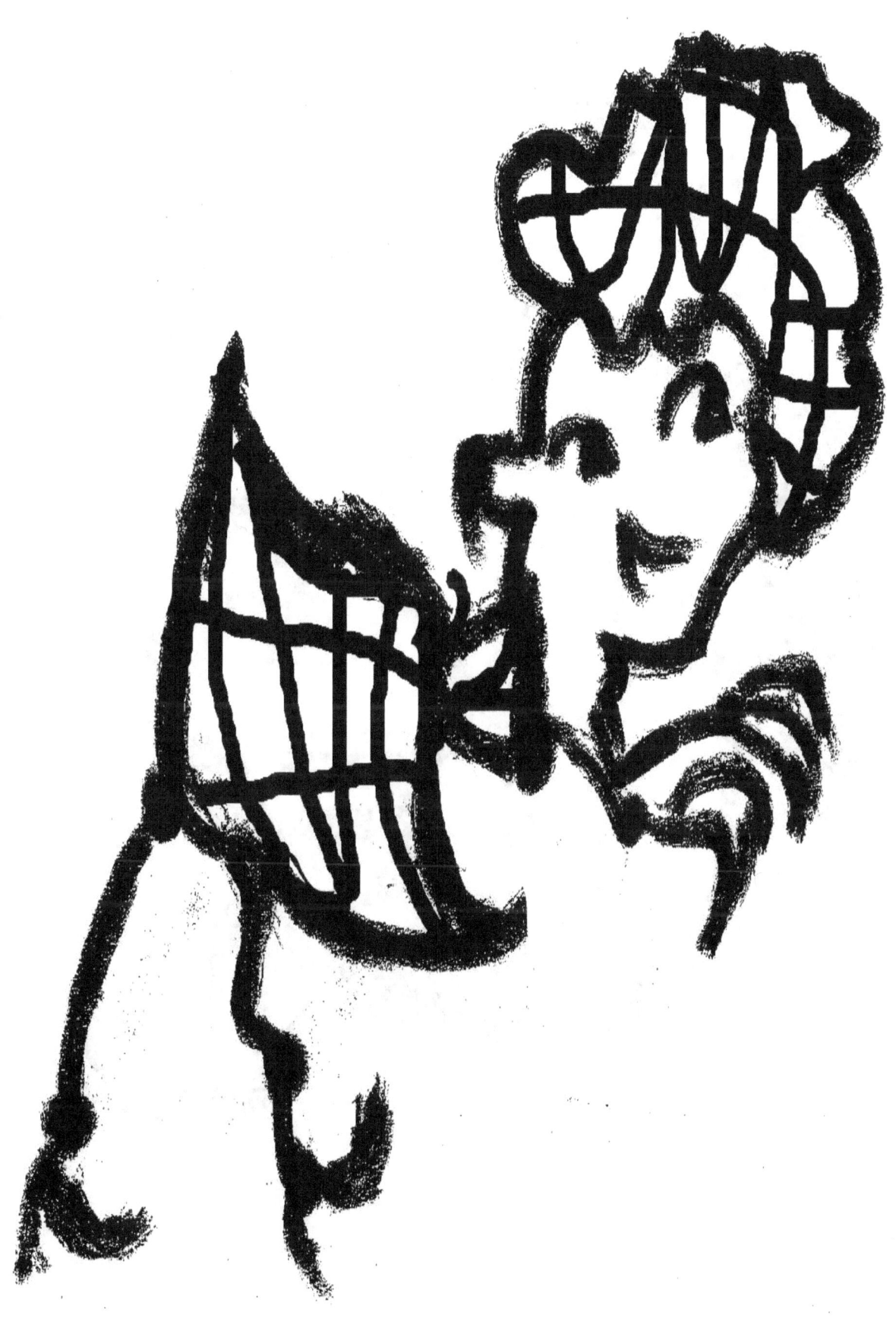

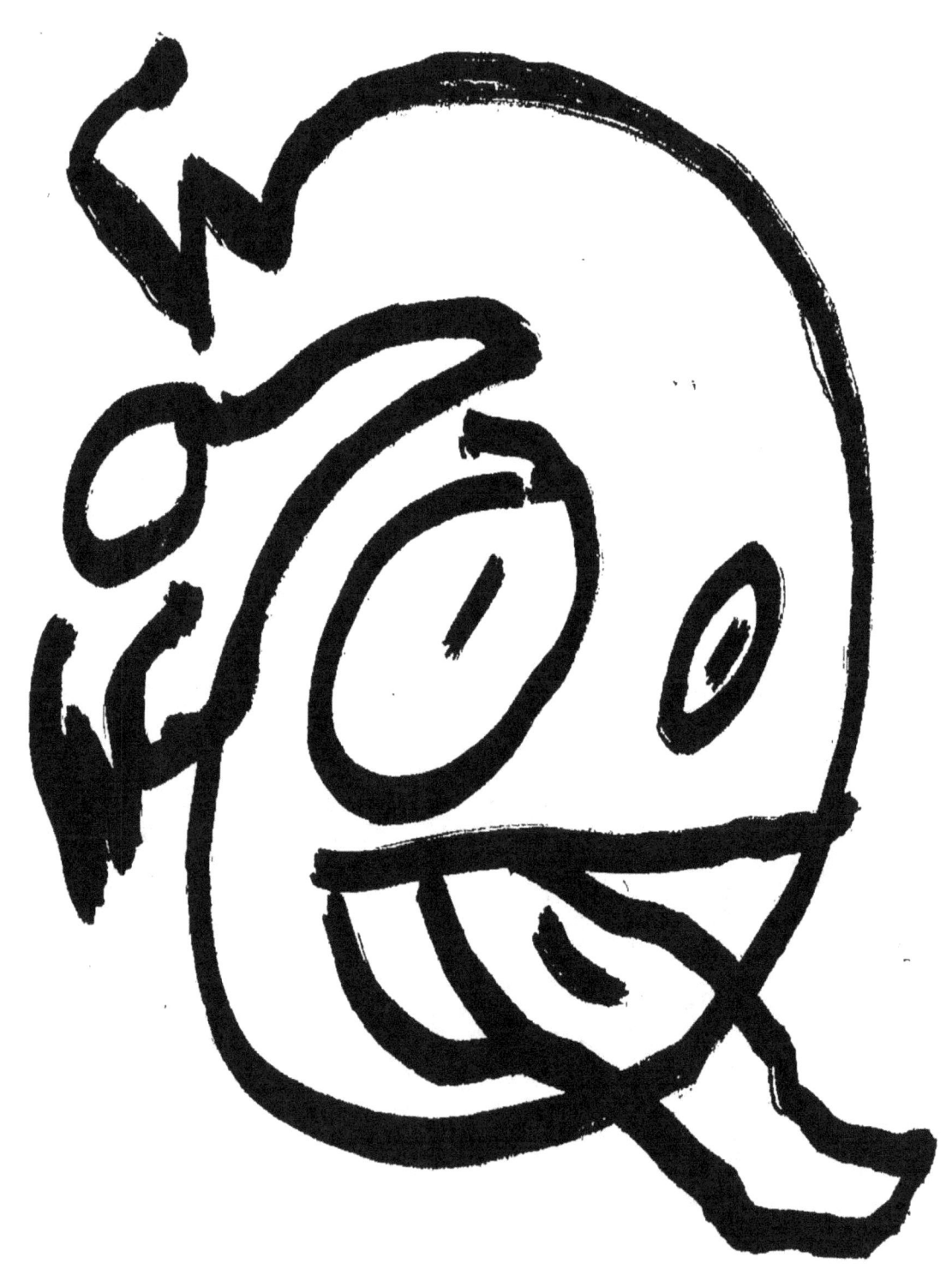

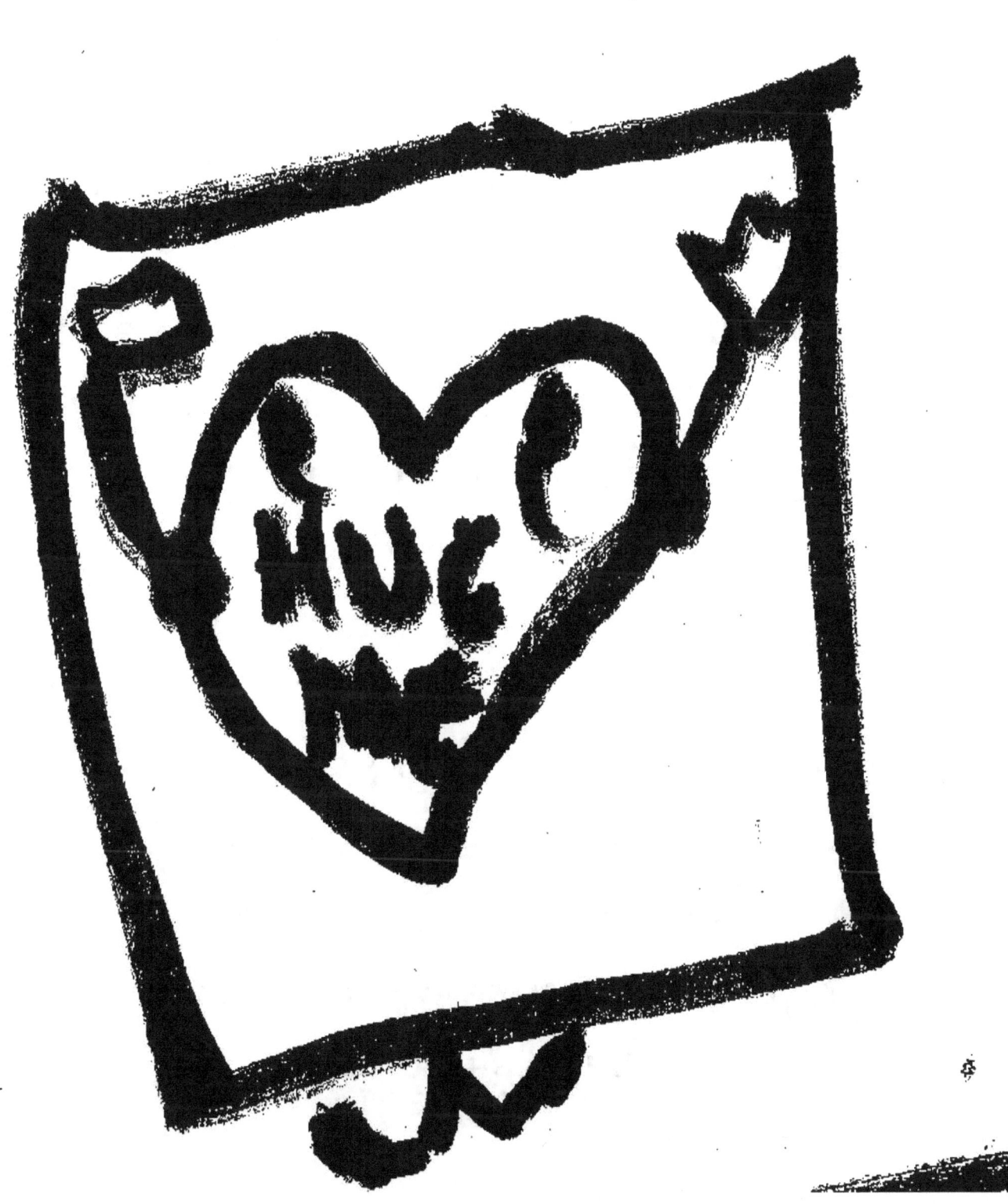

ABOUT THE AUTHOR

The author has a "**suparduparextraspectacularbinocularcoloring**" fascination with all kinds of art like Minnie's folk art. The author is from the dynasty of the late Uncle David Evans and Aunt Cecilia Evans of McClellanville—a Georgetown area in South Carolina.

ABOUT THE ARTIST

Art drawings are copyrighted and drawn by an emerging "USA Picasso" residing in the Deep South. The artist was formerly from a friendly, but alien world.

SPIRIT HAND CRAYONS

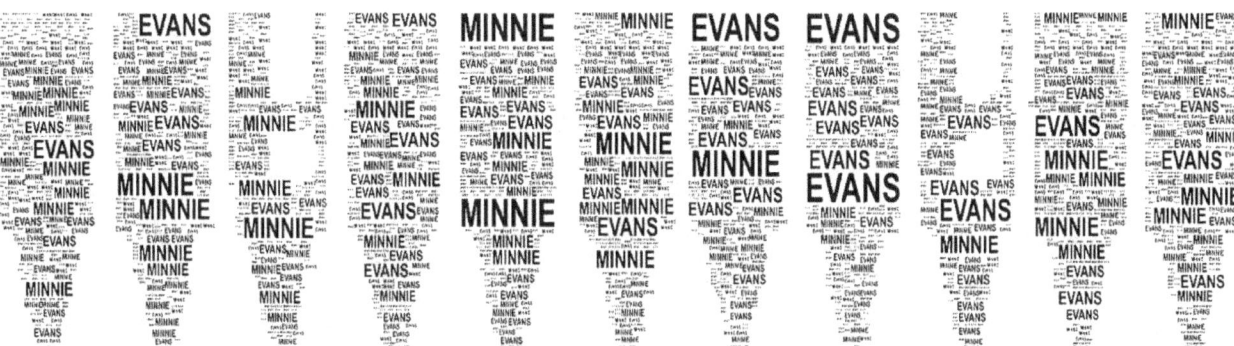

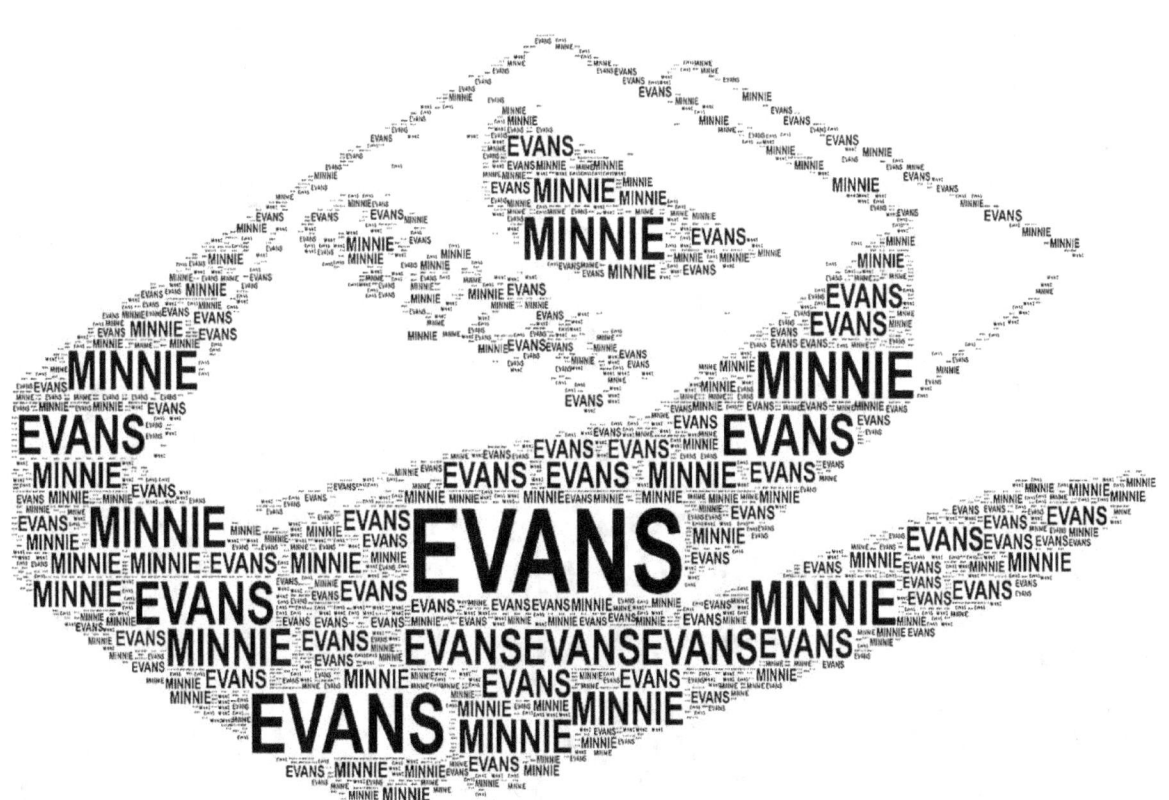

LIGHT SHINING FINE ART FRIENDS TREE

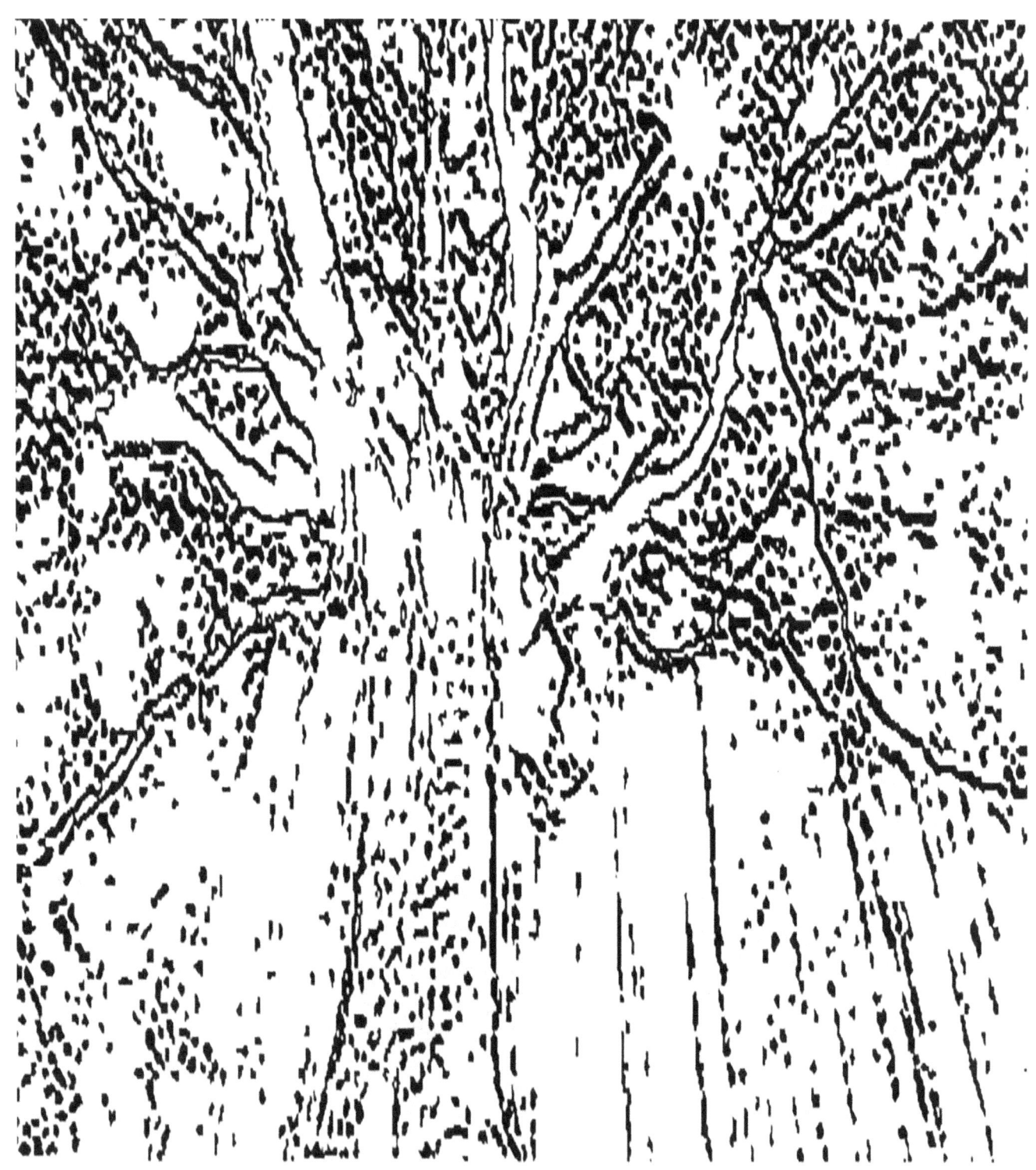

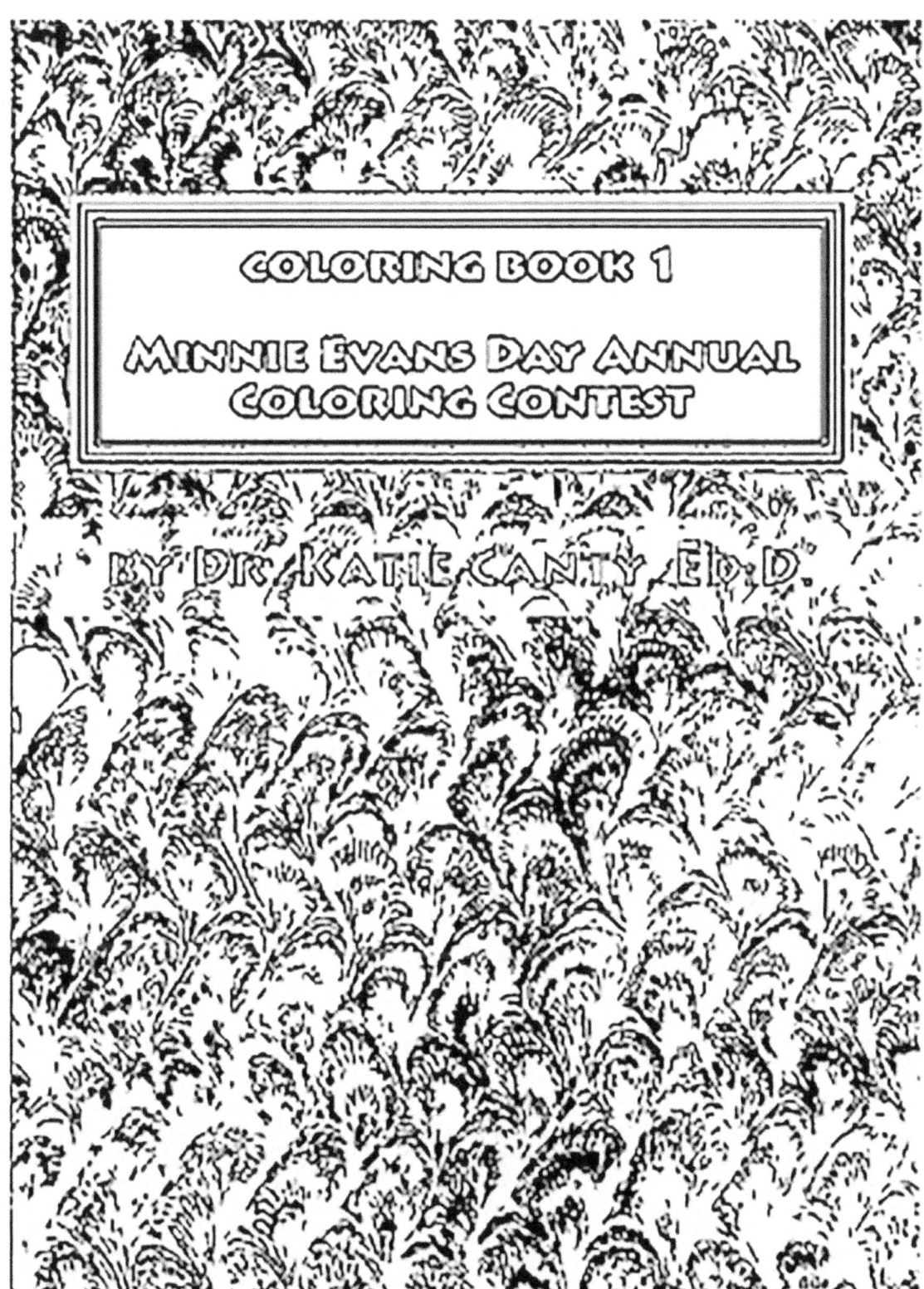

MEET MINNIE EVANS IN ONE SENTENCE

Compelled to draw by visions and dreams, Minnie Evans, a 25 cents a day, plantation gate keeper at age 47, suddenly and without stopping from 1935-1987, began attacking Coast Guard Station trashed paper with crayons and a spirit hand to yield hundreds of great-masters type, uncanny, sometimes scary, mathematically precise art works that are proving to be very valuable and highly sought after works of art.

7 RAREST UNSHARED FACTS ABOUT MINNIE'S 1892-1987 ERA

1. Born, raised, and lived in the lush forest and waterway areas surrounding Long Creek, NC—an area that to some could give the Amazon jungle a run for the money back there then in the early 1900's

2. A grown woman coloring during her spare time with kids crayons--less than in vogue back then

3. Expectation: be able to cook which includes a good pot of rice and gravy, keep the house very clean, work as a combo nanny/ domestic servant, be fruitful and multiply by having a son(s) to pass on the husband's family name

4. Art works angelic to many but frightening to some

5. Numerous artworks created on the Coast Guard trash paper tossed out by recipients as trash back then

6. Unsure as to whether she or her descendants profit financially from the sale of her highly sought after artworks

7. Rose above the many obstacles of her day to do what she felt God wanted her to do

http://www.amazon.com/-/e/B01MRY0HZX

http://beyondcomputerbasi.wix.com/coloringcontest

www.ingramcontent.com/pod-product-compliance
Lightning Source LLC
Chambersburg PA
CBHW062233220526
45471CB00009B/3456